新时代行业英语系列教材

总主编 姜 宏　　副主编 胡 霞 高亚妹
主 编 周欣奕　　原版作者 Luke Prodromou
　　　　　　　　　　　　　 Lucia Bellini

商务英语
ENGLISH for
Commerce

清華大学出版社
北 京

北京市版权局著作权合同登记号　图字：01-2021-1546

© licensed by ELI s.r.l, Italy — ELI Publishing.
www.elionline.com
Author: Luke Prodromou Lucia Bellini

The English adaptation rights arranged through Rightol Media. （本书英文改编版版权经由锐拓传媒取得）

图书在版编目（CIP）数据

商务英语 / 姜宏总主编；周欣奕主编. —北京：清华大学出版社，2021.4（2025.7 重印）
新时代行业英语系列教材
ISBN 978-7-302-57795-9

Ⅰ.①商…　Ⅱ.①姜…　②周…　Ⅲ.①商务–英语–高等职业教育–教材　Ⅳ.①F7

中国版本图书馆 CIP 数据核字（2021）第 055438 号

策划编辑：刘细珍
责任编辑：刘细珍
封面设计：子　一
责任校对：王凤芝
责任印制：丛怀宇

出版发行：清华大学出版社
　　　　网　　址：https://www.tup.com.cn，https://www.wqxuetang.com
　　　　地　　址：北京清华大学学研大厦 A 座　　　邮　编：100084
　　　　社 总 机：010-83470000　　　　　　　　邮　购：010-62786544
　　　　投稿与读者服务：010-62776969，c-service@tup.tsinghua.edu.cn
　　　　质 量 反 馈：010-62772015，zhiliang@tup.tsinghua.edu.cn
印 装 者：北京博海升彩色印刷有限公司
经　　销：全国新华书店
开　　本：210mm×285mm　　　印　张：8　　　　字　数：191 千字
版　　次：2021 年 4 月第 1 版　　　　　　　　印　次：2025 年 7 月第 3 次印刷
定　　价：55.00 元

产品编号：091251-02

在经济全球化和国际交往日益频繁的今天，无论是作为个人还是组织的一员，参与国际交流与合作都需要具备良好的外语沟通能力和扎实的专业技术能力。高职院校承担着培养具有全球竞争力的高端技术人才的使命，需要探索如何有效地培养学生的行业外语能力。行业外语教学一直是职业院校的短板，缺少合适的教材是其中一个主要原因。目前，国内大多数高职院校在第一学年开设公共英语课程，所用教材多为通用英语教材，其主题与学生所学专业的关联度总体较低；部分院校自主开发的行业英语教材，在专业内容的系统性、语言表达的准确性等方面存在诸多不足；还有部分院校直接采用国外原版的大学本科或研究生教材，但这些教材学术性和专业性太强，对以就业为导向的高职院校学生来说，十分晦涩难懂。

清华大学出版社从欧洲引进原版素材并组织国内一线行业英语教师改编的这套"新时代行业英语系列教材"，以提升学生职业英语能力为目标，服务师生教与学。本套教材具有如下特点：

一、编写理念突出全球化和国际化

本套教材在欧洲原版引进优质资源的基础上改编而成，全球化视角选材，结合行业领域和单元主题，关注环境保护、人口老龄化、贫困等时代难题，培养学生的国际视野和世界公民素养。单元主题、板块编排和练习设计与国际接轨，体现国际规范和国际标准，且反映全球行业发展动态和前景，帮助学生全面了解全球行业现状和掌握国际操作流程，夯实行业知识体系。

二、编写目标注重培养学生使用英语完成工作任务的实际应用能力

为响应高职院校外语教学改革号召，培养具有国际竞争力的高端技术人才，将外语教学目标由原来的语言能力导向转变为职业能力导向，本套教材通过听、说、读、写、译等基本语言技能训练，让学生完成不同行业领域的工作任务，将英语放到职场的背景中来学，放到员工的岗位职责、工作流程中来学。

三、结构与内容紧扣行业领域的职场情境和核心业务

本套教材围绕行业核心概念和业务组织教学单元，不同单元相互关联，内容由浅入深、由易到难，循序渐进；教材各单元主题契合行业典型工作场景，内容反映职业岗位核心业务知识与流程。每本教材根据内容设置 8 至 10 个单元，用多种形式的语言训练任务提升学生对行业知识的理解与应用。

四、资源立体多样，方便师生教与学

本套教材图文并茂。通过改编，在原版教材基础上每个单元增加了学习目标，明确了学生在完成各单元学习后应该达到的知识和能力水平；增加了重点词汇中文注释和专业术语表，便于学生准确理解行业核心概念；听力练习和阅读篇章均配有音频，并借助二维码扫码听音的形式呈现，实现教材的立体化，方便学生学习；习题安排契合单元的主题内容，便于检测单元学习目标的实现程度。教材另配有电子课件和习题答案，方便教师备课与授课。教师可以征订教材后联系出版社索取。

本套教材共10本，包括《护理英语》《机电英语》《建筑工程英语》《运输与物流英语》《烹饪、餐饮与接待英语》《旅游英语》《银行与金融英语》《市场营销与广告英语》《商务英语》《商务会谈英语》，涵盖医药卫生、机电设备、土木建筑、交通运输、旅游、财经商贸等六大类专业。建议高职院校结合本校人才培养目标，开设相应课程。

本套教材适合作为高职院校学生的行业英语教材，也适合相关行业从业人员作为培训或自学教材。

姜宏

2021年3月31日

本教材改编自意大利*Flash on English*系列引进教材。在原版教材的基础上，本教材增添了导入和术语两个模块，在原版听、说、读、写技能模块中添加单词释义，并进行适当的本土化改编，以适应我国高等职业教育学生的学习水平和需求。

从语言角度，本教材以提高国际商务英语能力为目标，在原汁原味的教学素材的基础上，根据跨国企业的真实岗位需要来设计听、说、读、写各环节语言任务，培养学生应对商务环境的英语语言能力。从专业角度，本教材通过介绍商务知识背景、培养商务专业技能、模拟商务工作流程完成专业训练，最后引导学生成功通过应聘面试走向涉外商务工作岗位。

本教材分为全球市场、商务公司、商务会话、电子邮件、市场营销、商业广告、贸易磋商、订单合同、贸易单据、应聘面试十个单元。全书带领学生了解全球市场、商务公司的专业背景，培养学生商务会话和电子邮件写作专业技能，通过制定市场营销策略及发布商业广告将产品推向市场，并完成贸易磋商、下订单签合同、制作贸易单据等贸易流程，最后辅导学生参加应聘面试。每个单元由导入模块、听、说、读、写技能模块和术语模块组成。导入模块通过热身活动激发学生兴趣和探知欲，从而更好地进入学习主题；技能模块开展听、说、读、写多方面的技能训练，通过增添单词释义帮助学生理解词汇，通过真实背景相关任务加强学生的英语语境沟通能力。听、说、读、写技能训练之间互相融合、互相促进；术语模块包含商务领域的相关拓展，以及国际商务专业知识指导。

本教材难易适中，语言素材规范，切合实际工作情境。本教材适合高等职业院校相关专业师生使用，同时也适用于相关行业从业人员培训或自学使用。

本教材由周欣奕、胡霞和高亚妹改编，周欣奕改编第一单元及第五至第九单元，胡霞改编第三、第四单元，高亚妹改编第二单元和第十单元。在本教材改编过程中得到北京财贸职业学院国际教育学院姜宏、闻立欧两位领导以及出版社同仁的大力支持和帮助，在此表示由衷感谢。由于编者水平所限，改编过程中难免存在不妥之处，敬请指正。

编者

2021年3月31日

Contents

Contents   v

Learning Objectives

Upon completion of the unit, students will be able to:

- identify goods and services;
- understand the definition and connotation of market;
- compare advantages and disadvantages of globalisation.

Starting Off

In this unit you may be studying the market. But do you know exactly what it is?

1 **Read the questionnaire below and tick (√) the best answers for you.**

The market	Yes	No	Don't know
1) may be the people who want to buy something.	☐	☐	☐
2) may be a place where many people can gather together to exchange goods and services.	☐	☐	☐
3) must be a real existing place or venue.	☐	☐	☐
4) involves producers, sellers, buyers and so on.	☐	☐	☐
5) only involves producers and consumers.	☐	☐	☐
6) must be a retail outlet, where people meet face-to-face.	☐	☐	☐
7) may be an online market, where there is no direct physical contact between buyers and sellers.	☐	☐	☐
8) may be where buyers and sellers are in contact with one another, either directly or through agents.	☐	☐	☐

The globalisation	Yes	No	Don't know
9) may be the procedure of cross-border interaction and integration among people, businesses, and governments.	☐	☐	☐
10) makes the world into a more interdependent place.	☐	☐	☐
11) eliminates all the barriers to trade.	☐	☐	☐
12) obtains the advantages integrated global economy, without any negative side-effect.	☐	☐	☐
13) may be the share of products, technology, information, and jobs across different cultures.	☐	☐	☐
14) can create economic growth by means of the worldwide flow of goods, capital, and labor.	☐	☐	☐
15) distributes economic growth and job creation fairly and evenly across industries or countries definitely.	☐	☐	☐
16) may reduce operating costs by manufacturing abroad, buy raw materials cheaply, and reach to new customers.	☐	☐	☐

Reading

Market

A **market** is where people buy and sell. The people who sell are called sellers—also **producers** or **manufacturers**—they make and **provide** what the market needs. The people who buy are called buyers—also **customers**—they use what they buy from sellers. But what is bought and sold in a market? Goods and services. Goods are **physical objects** like computers, mobile phones, shoes, **spaghetti**. Services are non-physical objects like **banking**, **transport**, **concerts**, **advertising**. Of course the **quantity** and type of goods and services produced interacts with the quantity and type of goods and services the market demands. This is called **the law of supply and demand**. The supply is the quantity of goods or services that producers put in the market. Demand is the **amount** of goods and services that buyers will buy. Producers make what consumers require because they don't want to produce something that nobody wants to buy. This law is the **driving force** of any market. But what influences a customer's choice of what product to buy and in what quantity? One of the most important factors that **determines** this choice is the price. In general, people buy more when the price is low and buy less when it is high. This can create **competition** in the market between different sellers of the same product who want to win as many customers as possible, so they must **beat competitors** but, at the same time, they must make a **profit**.

MY GLOSSARY

market	n.	市场; 行情; 销路	quantity	n. 数量, 量
producer	n.	生产者, 制作人; 发生器	the law of supply and demand	
manufacturer	n.	[经]制造商, 厂商		供求定理
provide	v.	提供; 规定; 准备	amount	n. 数量, 总数; 程度
customer	n.	顾客; 家伙	driving force	驱动力
physical objects		实物	determine	v. 下决心, 做出决定, 确定
spaghetti	n.	意大利式细面条	competition	n. 竞争, 比赛
banking	n.	银行业务; 银行业	beat	v. 打败; 打; 搅拌
transport	n.	运输; 运输机	competitor	n. 竞争者, 对手
concert	n.	音乐会, 演唱会	profit	n. 利润, 利益
advertising	n.	广告; 广告业		

2 Match the words and phrases on the left with their definitions on the right.

1) producer

2) customer

3) services

4) market

5) price

6) supply and demand

7) goods

8) advertising

a ☐ a place where buyers and sellers are in contact with one another

b ☐ the relationship between the quantity of products and services that are for sale and the quantity that people want to buy

c ☐ a company or person that makes goods

d ☐ things produced and sold

e ☐ someone who buys goods or services

f ☐ the amount of money you pay for something

g ☐ the activity of persuading people to buy something

h ☐ products which are not goods

3 Complete the sentences with words from the text.

1) The interaction of supply and _____ determines what is produced and the quantity.

2) Customers prefer buying products with a low _____.

3) FIAT is an Italian car _____.

4) Banking is a type of _____.

5) _____ is when sellers try to be more successful than others in a market.

6) Every company wants to have a _____ from its sales.

4 Label the pictures with the letter G (goods) or S (services).

1) _____ 2) _____ 3) _____ 4) _____ 5) _____

6) _____ 7) _____ 8) _____ 9) _____ 10) _____

5 **Read the interview with Paul Laxer, an MP3 player manufacturer. Complete the dialogue with the questions.**

> Does your company invest much in advertising
>
> ~~What exactly do you produce~~
>
> Do you mean that you beat the competition with low prices
>
> Is there much demand in the market for this type of product
>
> can we say that you're not worried about sales
>
> isn't there strong competition from mobile phones or smartphones

Interviewer:	So, Mr Laxer. Tell us something about your company. (1) *What exactly do you produce?*
Mr Laxer:	Well, we make MP3 players. We specialise in small, light, coloured, and of course, highly-technological MP3 players.
Interviewer:	(2) _____?
Mr Laxer:	Absolutely. At the beginning this product was just for young people. But now it's become very popular with older people as well. Today everybody listens to music anytime, anywhere.
Interviewer:	I agree with you but (3) _____? I mean, there are so many mobile phones with this function.
Mr Laxer:	It's true but still, our MP3 players have a good market. They have an unbeatable price compared to other similar articles and of course they're cheaper than good mobile phones.
Interviewer:	(4) _____?
Mr Laxer:	Yes, low prices combined with excellent quality, I would say.
Interviewer:	(5) _____?
Mr Laxer:	Not much. You see, our product has been on the market for a long time and has always been popular. So it's well-known and doesn't need too much advertising.
Interviewer:	So, (6) _____?
Mr Laxer:	Fortunately no, we aren't at the moment. But, you know, customers' needs may change at any time. We'll be ready when it happens.

Reading 2

Globalisation

Today we talk about the **global** market. This means that the whole world has become a single **marketplace** and is not formed by different national markets. In other words, we are in an **international** market where companies have more **opportunities** to sell their products in any country in the world and customers have more opportunities to buy products from all over the world. In international **economy** this is called globalisation: the process by which companies **operate** in a lot of different countries all around the world. What has **facilitated** this **process** of buying and selling in the world market? One of the most important factors is that, over the past 20 years, there have been **developments** in new **technology** and in **communication** systems: thanks to the use of the Internet, email, **mobile phones** and **video conferencing**, companies can communicate 24 hours a day, 7 days a week. Also, **improvements** in transport and the **reduction** in **restrictions** to commerce (**taxes** on **imports**, for example) have given companies more opportunities in foreign markets and have **contributed** to **free trade**.

MY GLOSSARY

globalisation	n.	全球化
global	adj.	全球的; 总体的; 球形的
marketplace	n.	市场, 商场, 市集
international	adj.	国际的; 国际通用的
opportunity	n.	机会, 时机
economy	n.	经济; 节约; 理财
operate	v.	经营; 操作; 开刀
facilitate	v.	促进; 帮助; 使容易
process	n.	过程, 工艺流程, 程序
development	n.	发展; 开发; 发育
technology	n.	技术, 工艺

communication	n.	交流; 通讯; 信函
mobile phone		手机, 移动电话
video conferencing		视频会议
improvement	n.	提高; 改进, 改善
reduction	n.	减少, 下降, 缩小
restriction	n.	限制, 约束, 束缚
tax	n.	税金; 重负
import	n.	进口; 输入
contribute	v.	有助于; 促成; 贡献
free trade		自由贸易

6 Read the text about globalisation and decide if the statements are true (*T*) or false (*F*). Correct the false statements.

	T	F
1) Globalisation can be defined as the activity of buying and selling goods and services in all the countries in the world.	☐	☐
2) Globalisation started in 1920.	☐	☐
3) Today people can communicate at any time on any day.	☐	☐
4) Taxes on imports is an example of free trade.	☐	☐
5) Today it is easier to transport goods from one country to another.	☐	☐

7 Translate the following sentences into Chinese.

1) In other words, we are in an international market where companies have more opportunities to sell their products in any country in the world and customers have more opportunities to buy products from all over the world.

2) One of the most important factors is that, over the past 20 years, there have been developments in new technology and in communication systems: thanks to the use of the Internet, email, mobile phones and video conferencing, companies can communicate 24 hours a day, 7 days a week.

8 Translate the following sentences into English.

1) 技术一直是全球化的主要推动力之一。

2) 全球化的支持者认为，全球化可以提高普通人的生活水平。

3) 全球化的反对者认为，自由市场以牺牲本土企业的利益为代价，令跨国公司受益。

9 Match the words on the left to the ones on the right which have similar meanings.

1) global   a ☐ limitation

2) facilitate   b ☐ exchange

3) development   c ☐ international

4) communication   d ☐ duty

5) tax   e ☐ improvement

6) restriction   f ☐ promote

Listening

10 Listen to the passage and then match the beginnings on the left and the ends on the right of sentences 1) to 3).

1) For you, as a customer, it means that   **a** ☐   he has earned more money.

2) For the disco's owner, it means that   **b** ☐   your choice is influenced by the costs of the two things you want to do.

3) For the cinema's owner, it means that   **c** ☐   he has lost a customer.

11 **Globalisation is a very controversial problem. Read the list below. Then, listen to two experts talking about it, and tick (√) the advantages and disadvantages of globalisation they mention.**

Advantages	Disadvantages
1) Poor countries can develop economically.	1) Only multinationals, like Coca Cola, get the benefits.
2) Poor countries can improve their standard of living.	2) Rich countries become richer at the expense of poor countries.
3) Globalisation is a force for democratic freedom.	3) Globalisation destroys the environment in poor countries.
4) Companies can sell more goods and make more money.	4) People who work for big multinationals are not well-paid.
5) Globalisation creates more jobs.	5) Multinationals invest in poor countries so there are fewer jobs in rich countries.
6) There is more circulation of money.	6) Multinationals control the economy of poor countries.
7) Because of strong competition, prices are lower.	7) Local cultures and traditions are not respected.
8) Thanks to globalisation, we know other cultures better.	8) Workers in poor countries are exploited.

Writing

12 **What's your opinion of globalisation? Write a text about it using the information from the text and the two boxes in Exercise 11. Follow the guidelines and use linkers and expressions from the box.**

Write what it is and how it has developed.

Write if you are in favour or against it and explain why.

First...   Then...   Also...   Finally...   I think that...   In my opinion...

Speaking

13 **Work in pairs. Ask and answer the following questions about market.**

1) Who is a seller and who is a buyer?

2) What is the difference between goods and services?

3) What is the difference between supply and demand?

4) Why is price an important factor in a market?

5) Do you agree that market demand influences what a producer puts in the market? Why?

Technical Terms

1 **Market** is a physical or virtual place where two parties can gather to exchange goods and services.

2 **Globalisation** is the spread of products, technology, information, and jobs across national borders and cultures.

3 **Market growth** is an increase in the number of people who buy a particular product or service, or the number of products, etc. that are sold.

4 **Market segment** is a group of possible customers who are similar in their needs, age, education, income, etc.

5 **Market segmentation** is the dividing of all possible customers into groups based on their needs, age, education, income, etc.

6 **Market share** is the number of products that a company sells compared with the number of items of the same type that other companies sell.

7 **Market research** is the collection and examination of information about things that people buy or might buy and their feelings about things that they have bought.

8 **Market economy** is an economic system in which goods and services are made, sold, and shared and prices set by the balance of supply and demand.

2 The Company

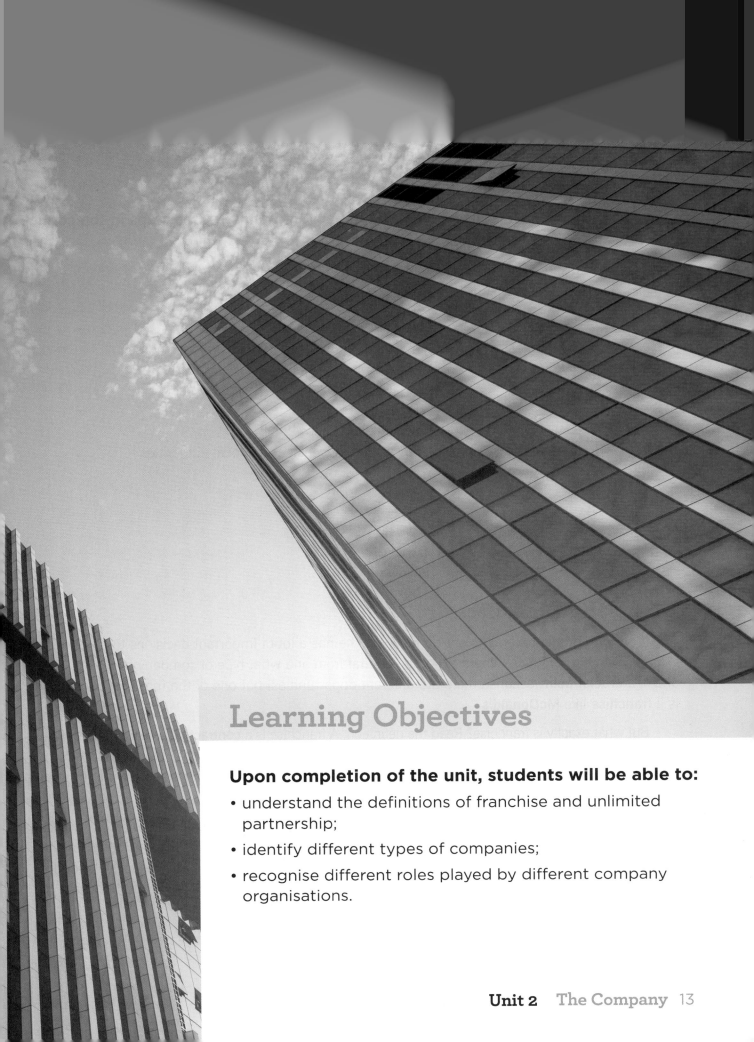

Learning Objectives

Upon completion of the unit, students will be able to:

- understand the definitions of franchise and unlimited partnership;
- identify different types of companies;
- recognise different roles played by different company organisations.

Starting Off

In this unit you may be studying the company. But do you know the process of starting a small company?

1 **Here are the steps of starting a small company in China. Put the steps in the correct order.**

- [ ] Open a business bank account
- [ ] Register for taxes at the State and Local Tax Bureau
- [ ] Decide business scope and conduct market research
- [ ] Register the business at any other relevant authorities
- [ ] Get the fund
- [ ] Write the business plan
- [ ] Determine the name, structure and location of the company
- [ ] Apply for Certificate of Approval and Business License at the local authorities

Reading 1

Company Classification

If an **entrepreneur** wants to start a business, he has a lot of important decisions to take — for example, what to produce, where to get the **capital** from and what type of company to **set up**. This one is a **crucial point** because there are different opportunities, but one of the most popular today is a **franchise** like **McDonald's**.

But what exactly is franchise? Read the definition. A franchise is a **contract** between two **parties** — the **franchisor** and the **franchisee**. The franchisee is a small business owner who sells goods or services produced by a large company, called the franchisor, in **exchange** for some **payment** (a **fee plus** a **percentage** of the profit).

Another form of business **organisation** is an **unlimited partnership**. It is formed by two or more owners (called **partners**) who **share** the **management** and **financial responsibility** for the business. This means that they take decisions together, share profits but are also responsible for the company's **debts**. What does that mean? It means that if the company goes **bankrupt**, they have to pay for the debts with their personal **possessions**.

Company Organisation

There are many things to be done in a company, for example: buy **materials**, produce the goods, **contact** and sell to **clients**, **administer** the company's **finances**. This is why there are different **departments** responsible for the various tasks.

The **structure** or organisation of a company can be **graphically** shown in an **organigram**, that is a **diagram representing** all departments. On top of this **chart** there is a **Board of Directors**, a group of people who control the company.

MY GLOSSARY

entrepreneur	n.	企业家; 承包人; 主办者
capital	n.	资金; 首都
set up		建立; 开业
crucial point		关键点, 重点; 要害
franchise	n.	特许经营; 特许权, 专营权
McDonald's	n.	麦当劳 (快餐品牌名)
contract	n.	合同
party	n.	当事人; 党派; 聚会
franchisor	n.	特许专营授权公司; 特许人
franchisee	n.	特许经营人; 有代销权的人或团体
exchange	n.	交换, 交流, 兑换
payment	n.	付款, 支付; 报酬; 报答
fee	n.	费用; 酬金
plus	prep.	加, 和
percentage	n.	百分比, 百分率, 百分数
organisation	n.	组织, 团体
unlimited partnership		无限责任合伙企业
partner	n.	合伙人, 伙伴; 配偶
share	v.	分担; 分享; 共用; 分配

management	n.	管理; 管理人员; 管理部门
financial	adj.	金融的; 财政的; 财务的
responsibility	n.	责任, 义务
debt	n.	债务; 借款; 罪过
bankrupt	adj.	破产的
possession	n.	财产; 拥有
material	n.	材料; 用具
contact	v.	联系, 接触
client	n.	客户, 顾客; 委托人
administer	v.	管理; 执行; 给予
finance	n.	财政; 金融
department	n.	部门; 系; 科; 局
structure	n.	结构, 构造
graphically	adv.	以图表形式地; 形象地; 逼真地; 清晰详细地
organigram	n.	组织结构图, 构造示意图, 组织系统图
diagram	n.	图表; 图解
represent	v.	表现; 代表
chart	n.	图表; 海图; 图纸
Board of Director		董事会

2 Think of a franchise restaurant or store you know. What are its characteristics? Circle Yes or No.

1)	They sell the same products/goods.	Yes	No
2)	You can't find them in different towns and countries.	Yes	No
3)	Prices are similar in different countries.	Yes	No
4)	They have the same logo.	Yes	No
5)	They never have the same shop furniture.	Yes	No
6)	They use different types of advertising.	Yes	No

3 Choose the best alternative to complete the sentences.

1) _____ provides the logo. A. Franchisor B. Franchisee

2) _____ sells a well-known product. A. Franchisor B. Franchisee

3) _____ invests in research and promotion. A. Franchisor B. Franchisee

4) _____ has a network of outlets in different geographical areas. A. Franchisor B. Franchisee

5) _____ uses a famous trademark. A. Franchisor B. Franchisee

6) _____ is obliged to buy exclusively from one company. A. Franchisor B. Franchisee

7) _____ has the exclusive right to sell those goods in his geographical area. A. Franchisor B. Franchisee

8) The new Coca Cola _____ campaign is fantastic. A. company B. advertising

9) Mr Johnson is the _____ of this restaurant. A. owner B. trademark

10) Please send the _____ by train. A. profit B. goods

11) We want to _____ a new company. A. set up B. provide

12) IKEA has a lot of _____ in Europe. A. outlets B. business

13) I hope I become a successful _____. A. fee B. entrepreneur

4 Read the text and answer the questions. And then match the words and phrases on the left with their definitions on the right.

1) Who forms an unlimited partnership?

_____

2) What are the members of an unlimited partnership called?

_____

3) What are the advantages of this type of business organisation?

_____

4) What is the disadvantage?

_____

5) profit   **a** ☐ shop

6) trademark   **b** ☐ sum of money that you have to pay

7) go bankrupt   **c** ☐ the money that remains after paying costs

8) outlet   **d** ☐ name of a product than can't be used by any other company

9) debts   **e** ☐ to be unable to pay your debts

5 **These are some basic departments. Can you choose what each of the departments does from the box below?**

> buys all materials necessary for production
> organises advertising and product promotion
> looks after the company staff
> deals with the company's financial matters
> is responsible for selling what the company produces
> makes the products

1) production department _____

2) sales department _____

3) finance department _____

4) human resources department _____

5) marketing department _____

6) purchasing department _____

Reading 2

Richard Turner's Career

When he was 21, Richard Turner started working as an **accountant** for a mobile phone company. "I sat at my **PC** in the office and **checked** the **invoices** and payments all day, every day. I didn't like my job—it was so **boring** and **repetitive**. But I was **ambitious**: I wanted to gain experience in the **accounting** field and maybe have my own business one day," he says. So, he stayed in the company for about 10 years with no hope of **progressing** in his **career**.

One day, he went to a party and met Brian Harris, an old **schoolmate**. Brian was an **agent**—he worked for a company called GameWorld **Ltd** which produced **video games**. They talked for a while and Richard told Brian that he wasn't happy with his job. His friend said that his company was looking for somebody to work in the Finance Department, so Richard **applied for** the post. He sent his **CV** and went for an **interview**.

In a couple of months he was an accountant at GameWorld Ltd. The **atmosphere** was completely different: it was a **dynamic** company where people could take the **initiative** and progress in their careers. Besides, in five years, the company grew **considerably**, controlling about 30% of the market in England.

Richard became the Finance Department manager two years ago. "I still work on everything **related to** money, that is **expenditure** and costs," he says. "But the difference is that now I don't do it personally—I **coordinate** a team that checks invoices and payments like I used to do!"

MY GLOSSARY

accountant	*n.*	会计师, 会计人员
PC	*abbr.*	个人电脑 (Personal Computer)
check	*v.*	检查, 核对
invoice	*n.*	发票; 发货单
boring	*adj.*	无聊的; 令人厌烦的
repetitive	*adj.*	重复的

ambitious	*adj.*	野心勃勃的, 有雄心的
accounting	*n.*	会计; 会计学; 账单
progress	*v.*	进步; 进行; 前进
career	*n.*	事业; 职业生涯
schoolmate	*n.*	同学, 同窗
agent	*n.*	代理商, 代理人

Ltd	abbr.	有限责任公司（Limited）	dynamic	adj.	有活力的; 动态的; 动力的
video game		电子游戏; 电视游戏	initiative	n.	主动权; 首创精神; 新方案; 倡议
apply for		申请, 请求			
CV	abbr.	简历（Curriculum Vitae）	considerably	adv.	相当地, 非常地
			relate to		涉及; 有关
interview	n.	面试; 面谈; 接见; 采访	expenditure	n.	支出, 花费; 经费; 消费额
atmosphere	n.	气氛; 大气; 空气	coordinate	v.	配合; 调节

6 Match the words on the left to their definitions on the right.

1) accountant   **a** ☐ a document showing how much you owe someone for goods or services

2) invoice   **b** ☐ the total amount of money that people or organisations spend during a period of time

3) apply   **c** ☐ a meeting in which someone asks you questions to see if you are suitable for a job

4) interview   **d** ☐ to make a formal request

5) expenditure   **e** ☐ someone whose job is to keep and check financial accounts

7 Choose the best title for each paragraph.

1) Richard's recent successful career   Paragraph _____

2) Richard's first job   Paragraph _____

3) His start at GameWorld Ltd.   Paragraph _____

4) A fantastic job opportunity   Paragraph _____

8 Decide if the statements are true (T) or false (F).

1) Richard worked for his first company for about 10 years. _____

2) He didn't like his first job but he had no ambition. _____

3) He heard about the post in the Finance Department at GameWorld Ltd. from a newspaper. _____

4) The new company was better than the old one. _____

5) He became a manager as soon as he started working for GameWorld Ltd. _____

9 Translate the following sentences into Chinese.

1) "I sat at my PC in the office and checked the invoices and payments all day, every day. I didn't like my job—it was so boring and repetitive. But I was ambitious: I wanted to gain experience in the accounting field and maybe have my own business one day," he says.

----

2) "I still work on everything related to money, that is expenditure and costs," he says. "But the difference is that now I don't do it personally—I coordinate a team that checks invoices and payments like I used to do!"

Listening

10 Listen to two entrepreneurs talking about their businesses and complete the table.

Name of company		
When it was set up		
Type of business		
Advantages		
Disadvantages		

11 This is the organigram of an English company called **F&M Ltd.** Listen to some managers who work there and complete the chart with their names in the correct department.

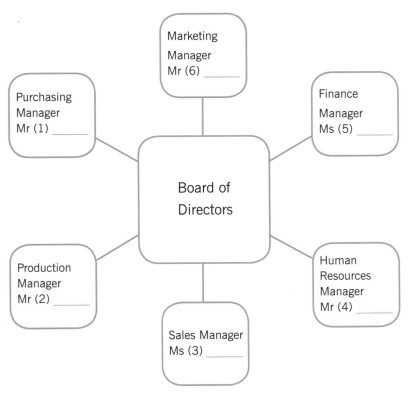

Marketing
Manager
Mr (6) _____

Purchasing
Manager
Mr (1) _____

Finance
Manager
Ms (5) _____

Board of
Directors

Production
Manager
Mr (2) _____

Human
Resources
Manager
Mr (4) _____

Sales Manager
Ms (3) _____

Writing

12 Write a summary of Reading 2 including the information below (about 100 words).

— what his first job was, whether he liked it and why

— why he applied for the post at GameWorld Ltd.

— why he liked working there

— what career progression he had at GameWorld Ltd

— what his present responsibilities are

_____

_____

_____

_____

_____

_____

Speaking

13 **Go back to all the information about franchises and unlimited partnerships and prepare a presentation following the guidelines below:**

— name and definition of the people involved

— their duties/responsibilities

— the reason(s) why you think you would(n't) like to set one up

These sentences may help you:

> The people involved in _____ are called _____.
>
> These are their/his responsibilities/duties: _____.
>
> I would(n't) like to set up a _____ because _____.

Technical Terms

1 **Company** is an organisation that sells goods or services in order to make money.

2 **Franchise** is a type of license to grant a franchisee access to a franchisor's proprietary business knowledge, processes and trademarks, and a right to allow the franchisee to sell a product or service under the franchisor's business name.

3 **Sole proprietorship** is owned and operated by a single person.

4 **Partnership** is owned by two or more people who share responsibilities and profits.

5 **Limited partnership (LP)** exists when two or more partners go into business together, but one or more of the partners are only liable up to the amount of their investment. The general partner of the LP has unlimited liability.

6 **Limited liability partnership (LLP)** allows for a partnership structure where each partner's liabilities is limited to the amount they put into the business.

7 **Unlimited partnership** is owned by two or more people who share responsibilities and profits, and the legal liabilities of all the members are not limited.

Learning Objectives

Upon completion of the unit, students will be able to:

- speak over the phone;
- fix appointments and organise meetings;
- discuss issues, compare different opinions and reach an agreement.

Starting Off

In this unit you may be studying business conversation. But do you know how to exchange opinions? Working in a company also means discussing issues, comparing different opinions and reaching an agreement.

1 **Make a discussion with the help of the following sentences.**

Asking for opinions	Expressing opinions	Agreeing and disagreeing
What do you think about (that)?	I think that...	I agree with you.
		I think you're right.
What's your opinion of (that)?	I'm sure that...	I don't know. / I'm not sure about that.
		I don't think you're right.
		I'm sorry but I don't agree.
		I disagree (completely).

Reading 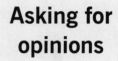 1

Using Business English does not only involve reading or writing emails, **documents**, or contracts but also speaking about **business matters** with other people.

Phone Calls

When you work in a company, a lot of your work is done over the telephone, so being able to speak over the phone is a **fundamental** skill in business.

Fixing Appointments

One of the reasons people speak over the phone is to **fix appointments** and organise meetings.

2 **Translate the following sentences into Chinese.**

1) Right. I'll give him your message. _____

2) I'm sorry but the line is busy. _____

3) Thank you. Goodbye. _____

4) Can I speak to Jack Barnes, please? _____

5) Would you like to leave a message? _____

6) Yes, please. I'll hold. _____

3 **Look at this list of typical sentences used when speaking on the phone and fill in the gaps with sentences from Exercise 2.**

Receiver	Caller
Brown Ltd, good morning. Can I help you?	Good morning. This is Ted Lee from Kelly & Sons.
Just a moment. I'll put you through.	(1) _____
I'm sorry but Mr Parker is not in the office.	Yes, please. Can you ask him to call me back, please?
(2) _____	(4) _____
(3) _____	It's OK, thanks. I'll call back later.
Would you like to hold?	(6) _____
(5) _____	
Right. I'll get him to call you back.	
All right. I'll tell him that you called.	
Thank you for calling. Goodbye.	

4 Can you complete the translations of these typical questions and answers? When you finish, check the answers with your partner.

> **A:** Can we/I'd like to fix an appointment. (?)
> (1) _____
>
> **B:** Yes, certainly. Let me get my diary.
> (2) _____

B: Is Tuesday at 10 OK for you?
(3) _____

A: I'm afraid I'm busy. Shall we meet on / What about Tuesday afternoon, instead?
(4) _____

B: Yes, that's fine. Shall we make it 3 o'clock?
(5) _____

A: OK. I'll see you on Tuesday at 3 in your office, then.
(6) _____

B: When would be convenient for you?
(7) _____

A: I'm free on Friday morning.
(8) _____

B: OK. What time shall we meet?
(9) _____

A: Shall we say at 10?/Would 10 be OK for you?
(10) _____

B: That's fine. See you on Friday at 10 in your office, then.
(11) _____

Reading 2

Dialogue 1

Paul: So, let's talk about these **proposals** for our new **advertising campaign**. What do you think about it, Liz?

Liz: I think the **TV ad** is really great but the photos used for the **advertisement** on our **website** are terrible.

Jason: I agree with you. I mean, about the photos, I don't like them either. But I'm not sure the TV ad is good. I think it's too long.

Paul: Yes, I think you're right. The TV ad should be shorter. But I think that the online advertisement is **fantastic**—photos included. Anyway, what's your opinion of the **gadgets**? I think they're "special". Do you agree?

Jason:	Absolutely. I agree completely.
Liz:	Well, I'm sorry but I don't agree. We should find something better.

Dialogue 2

A	Ann:	As you know, a new **Swedish** customer, FCF **Corporation**, has just contacted us for a very large order of our **crash helmets**. We have to discuss what terms to give him. I mean **price**, **discount** and **payment terms**. Let's start with price. What do you think?
B	Alex:	I agree with you. So let's tell him that we can't and ask him to pay when he receives the goods.
C	Ann:	Yes, Alex, I think you're right. It's a good price. But his order is very large, so I think we should give him a good discount, let's say 15%.
D	Ann:	OK, 10% then. Now, he asks to pay after 30 days. I'm sure that we've never given these terms to any of our customers for their first order.
E	Alex:	I don't agree. 15% is too high. Let's make it 10%.
F	Ann:	All right. I agree. I'll send him an email immediately.
G	Alex:	Well, I don't think we should change our **catalogue** price which is very **competitive**.

MY GLOSSARY

proposal	n.	建议; 计划; 提案
advertising campaign		广告战
TV ad		电视广告
advertisement	n.	广告; 启事
website	n.	网站
fantastic	adj.	极好的
gadgets	n.	小器具, 小装置, 小玩意儿
absolutely	adv.	一点不错, 完全对
completely	adv.	完全地, 彻底地; 十分地

Swedish	adj.	瑞典的; 瑞典语的
corporation	n.	大公司, 集团公司
crash helmet	n.	防护头盔, 安全帽
price	n.	价格
discount	n.	折扣, 减价, 打折
payment terms		付款条件
catalogue	n.	（商品）目录册
competitive	adj.	具有竞争力的

5 Read Dialogue 1 and complete the table. Tick (√) the things they like and put a cross (×) for the things they don't like.

	Paul	Liz	Jason
TV ad			
website advert			
gadgets			

6 Read Dialogue 2 and put the sentences A–G in the correct order.

1) ☐   2) ☐   3) ☐   4) ☐   5) ☐   6) ☐   7) ☐

7 Translate Dialogue 1 into Chinese.

_____

_____

_____

_____

_____

_____

8 Translate Dialogue 2 into Chinese with the right order.

_____

_____

_____

_____

_____

_____

Listening

9 Listen to Phone Call 1 and complete it with the missing words and phrases and then listen to Phone Call 2 and complete the memo.

Phone Call 1

Operator: (1) _____. Delta Limited. Can I help you?

Karen Mills: Ah, yes, good morning. (2) _____ Karen Mills from Jenkins Marketing. (3) _____ Jan Dixon, please?

Operator: Good morning, Mrs Mills. (4) _____. I'll put you through... I'm sorry, Mrs Mills, but (5) _____. Would you like to hold or (6) _____?

Karen Mills: I'll leave a message. Can you ask him to (7) _____, please? I'd like to ask him a few questions about his last order.

Operator: No problem. I'll (8) _____ to call you back as soon as he's free. Thanks (9) _____. Goodbye.

Karen Mills: Thank you. (10)_____.

Phone Call 2

ARTTOUCH LTD.

To:	(11) _____
Name of caller:	(12) _____
Company:	(13) _____
Phone number:	(14) _____
Message:	(15) _____

10 Listen to a phone call between Brett Collins and Sarah Young and choose the correct alternative.

1) Brett Collins...

   A. wants to speak to Sarah Young.

   B. receives a phone call from Sarah Young.

2) ...wants to fix an appointment.

   A. Brett

   B. Sarah

3) Brett is...

   A. free on Monday and Wednesday afternoon.

   B. busy

4) They decide to meet on...

   A. Monday.

   B. Wednesday.

5) They will meet at...

   A. 5.

   B. 3.

Writing

11 Write the dialogue following the instructions.

Operator: *(Answer the phone. The name of your company is Martins Electronics.)*

_____

Henry Palmer: *(Greet. Say your name. You work for Olsen Ltd. You want to speak to Matt Russell.)*

_____

Operator: *(Ask him to hold. Put Matt Russell through.)*

_____

Henry Palmer: *(Thank him.)*

_____

Matt Russell: *(Greet Mr Palmer. Ask him how he is.)*

_____

Henry Palmer: *(You are fine, now ask him.)*

_____

Matt Russell: *(You are fine. Ask him what you can do for him.)*

_____

Henry Palmer: *(You want to fix an appointment for the next month. Suggest Wednesday 18th.)*

_____

Matt Russell: *(You are busy. Suggest Friday 20th.)*

_____

Henry Palmer: *(Accept. Ask him morning or afternoon.)*

_____

Matt Russell: *(Suggest 9 in the morning in your office.)*

_____

Henry Palmer: *(You have another appointment at 9. Suggest 11.)*

_____

Matt Russell: *(Accept. Repeat the details of the appointment.)*

_____

Henry Palmer: *(Confirm. Thank. Say goodbye.)*

_____

Matt Russell: *(Thank. Say goodbye.)*

_____

Speaking

12 Tom White works for a company called Scott Bikes. He calls one of his customers, Action Sports, and asks to speak to Alice Ellis. The operator connects him but then says that the line is engaged. He say she'll call back later. Complete the dialogue.

Operator: Good morning. (1) _____?

Tom White: Good morning. (2) _____.

Operator: Just (3) _____. I'll (4) _____ … I'm sorry (5) _____. Would you like (6) _____?

Tom White: It's (7) _____.

Operator: OK, Mr White. I'll tell Mrs Ellis that (8) _____.

Tom White: Thanks.

Operator: Thank you for (9) _____.

Tom White: (10) _____.

Technical Terms

1 **Telephone etiquettes** are the rules of what should do or avoid, to communicate by phone successfully. The rules are as follows:

- answer the call immediately;
- identify yourself;
- speak politely;
- listen carefully;
- take notes;
- use proper volume;
- remain cheerful;
- be honest and sincere.

2 **Voicemail etiquettes** are the rules of how to leave a professional voicemail phone message which reflect your company's image.

- identify yourself;
- say your phone number twice;
- tell the reasons for calling;
- give reasons to call back;
- repeat and spell your name.

Learning Objectives

Upon completion of the unit, students will be able to:

- understand the meaning of each part in a business email;
- know the rules about language, style and structure of a business email;
- write a business email in a standard format.

Starting Off

In this unit you may be studying email. The most common form of written communication in business is email (electronic mail). Therefore, the ability to use email well is very important for anybody working in a company. If you already use emails to communicate with friends, you know how many advantages it has.

1 **This is a list of some advantages of communicating by email. Match the beginnings of the sentences on the left to the endings on the right.**

1) Sending emails is fast and

2) You can send emails anytime and

3) You can attach files

4) You can send emails wherever you are

5) You can send the same email to

6) Using emails saves the time of printing, copying and

7) You can store your emails and find them quickly when

a ☐ (no matter how "heavy" they are).

b ☐ a large number of people.

c ☐ you need them.

d ☐ distributing information to many people.

e ☐ simple.

f (but you must have a computer or a smart phone).

g ☐ anywhere.

Reading 1

Email Format

Like any document, an email has a **standard format**: it is organised in different parts.

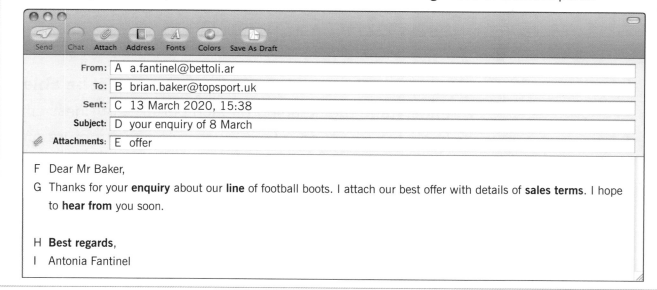

From: A a.fantinel@bettoli.ar
To: B brian.baker@topsport.uk
Sent: C 13 March 2020, 15:38
Subject: D your enquiry of 8 March
Attachments: E offer

F Dear Mr Baker,

G Thanks for your **enquiry** about our **line** of football boots. I attach our best offer with details of **sales terms**. I hope to **hear from** you soon.

H **Best regards,**

I Antonia Fantinel

standard	*adj.*	标准的; 合规格的
format	*n.*	格式; 版式
subject	*n.*	标题; 主题; 起因; 科目
attachment	*n.*	附件; 附着
enquiry	*n.*	询盘, 询问

line	*n.*	类别; 路线; 航线; 排; 绳
sales term		销售术语
hear from		收到······的信
best regards		诚挚的问候; 最好的祝福; 致敬

2 Look at the email in reading 1 and label the parts A–I correctly.

- ☐ **1)** salutation (=the receiver's name)
- ☐ **2)** complimentary closing (=the sender's regard for the receiver)
- ☐ **3)** email address of the receiver (=the address which receives the email)
- ☐ **4)** subject (=information about the content of the email)
- ☐ **5)** signature (=the sender's name)
- ☐ **6)** enclosure (=anything attached to the email)
- ☐ **7)** email address of the sender (=the address which sends the email)
- ☐ **8)** body of the message (=the main parts of the email)
- ☐ **9)** date and time (=specific time when the email is sent)

3 Read the email again and answer the questions.

1) Who writes the email and who does she work for?

_____

2) Who receives the email and who does he work for?

_____

3) When is the email sent?

_____

4) What is attached to the email?

_____

5) Why does Mrs Fantinel write the email?

_____

4 **Now complete this text summarising the email in Reading 1.**

On (1) _____ at (2) _____ Mrs (3) _____ from
(4) _____ sent an email to (5) _____ from (6) _____.
She thanked him for (7) _____ and attached (8) _____.

5 **Put the following sentences into the right parts of the body of an email (Four Point Plan).**

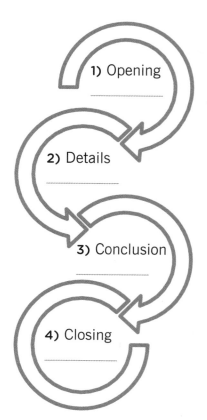

A For the past two years, I have worked as an assistant manager for ABC Company.

B Thank you in advance for your cooperation.

C We regret to learn from your letter that…

D Please let me have full details of the price involved together with the catalogue.

E Your early reply will be highly appreciated.

F I have learned your name and address from the ad on line.

G Hope to hear from you soon.

H Thank you for your letter of…

I If payment is not received within three days, this matter will be placed in the hands of our solicitor.

J The anniversary ceremony will be held on Friday, October the fourth.

K We are pleased to reply to your letter of…

L Cocktails will be served promptly at six to be followed by dinner at eight.

M I recommend him enthusiastically.

N With reference to your letter of…, we…

O We have received your letter of…

P We look forward to your early reply with much interest.

Q As this position requires excellent communication skills, my ability to speak both French and English fluently would be a definite asset for your company.

R A prompt reply would be appreciated.

Reading 2

Writing Rules

When you write an email you must **follow some rules** about **language**, **style** and structure. These questions can help you write the **perfect** email.

1) Is the **message** short and clear?
2) Are **grammar** and **spelling** correct?
3) Are the attachments **mentioned** in the message **attached**?
4) Are **paragraphs separated** by a line space?
5) Is the subject included and is it clear?
6) Does the body **contain** all standard parts (**opening**, **body**, **closing** and **signature**)?

From: tina.richardson@fandsons.uk
To: j.owens@citybank.com
Sent: 8 August 2020, 08:12
Subject:
Attachments:

Dear Mrs Owens,
Following our telepone conversation, I would like to fix an appointment for next 20 August at 10, if that is OK for you.
I have attach the documents we will discuss together.
Please **confirm** our appointment.
Best regards,
Tina richardson

MY GLOSSARY

follow the rules		遵守规则
language	n.	语言; 语言文字
style	n.	风格, 类型
perfect	adj.	完美的, 最好的
message	n.	消息; 差使
grammar	n.	语法
spelling	n.	拼写; 拼字; 拼法
mention	v.	提到, 谈到, 提及
attach	v.	附加, 附属

paragraph	n.	段落; 短评
separate	v.	隔开, 分离, 分开
contain	v.	包含; 容纳
opening	n.	开头语; 开始; 机会
body	n.	正文; 主要部分, 主体; 身体
closing	n.	结束语; 关闭; 倒闭
signature	n.	签字, 署名; 信号
confirm	v.	确认, 确定; 证实; 批准

6 Read the email in Reading 2. Answer the questions and take notes of your answers to decide if it is a "perfect" email or not.

1) Is the message short and clear?

_____

2) Are grammar and spelling correct?

_____

3) Are the attachments mentioned in the message attached?

_____

4) Are paragraphs separated by a line space?

_____

5) Is the subject included and is it clear?

_____

6) Does the body contain all standard parts (opening, body, closing and signature)?

_____

7 Rewrite the email in Reading 2 correctly.

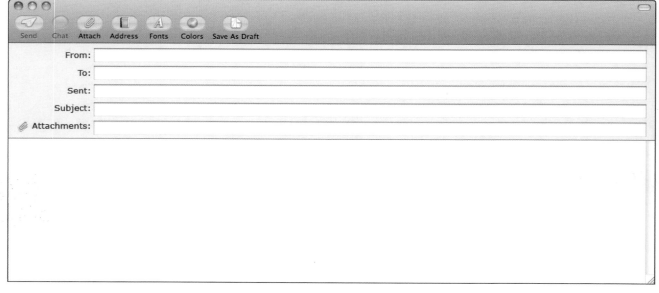

8 Translate the following sentences into Chinese.

1) I am sorry to learn from your letter of 12 Dec. that you have not been ready to effect shipment right now.

_____

2) We are the biggest dealer in London, and have branches in fifteen countries.

_____

3) Would you please send us a copy of your catalogue with current price and detailed specification?

_____

4) May the trade connections between our companies continue to develop with each passing day!

_____

9 **Translate the following sentences into English.**

1) 感谢你昨天来信邀请我参加贵公司成立20周年庆典。

_____

2) 我写这封电子邮件的目的是衷心祝贺你们取得的非凡成就。

_____

3) 如果你们的产品质量使我们满意，并且价格合理，我们将大量订货。

_____

4) 我怀着极大的兴趣期待着你的早日答复。

_____

Listening

10 **Why do business people use emails? Listen to this interview with a businessman and find 4 reasons he gives for using email.**

He uses email:

1) to _____ and _____

2) to _____

3) to _____ or _____

4) to _____

11 Listen to a businesswoman dictating an email to her secretary and complete the email.

From: clare.taylor@globalnet.com
To: (1) _____
Sent: 10 July 2020, 11:45
Subject: (2) _____
Attachments: (3) _____

Dear (4) _____,

Thanks for (5) _____ of
(6) _____.
Unfortunately I have to (7) _____ of
2 August as I have another (8) _____. Can
we meet on 3 August at (9) _____?

I look forward to your reply.
Best regards,
Clare (10) _____

Writing

12 Complete the email according to the following situation.

On 5th November 2020, at 2:32 in the afternoon, Carmen Lopez (c.lopez@garcia.com) sends an email to one of her customers, Dario Randi (dario.randi@marcolongo.it) to thank him for his order of 27th October. She attaches the details of their sales terms and asks for confirmation before sending the material.

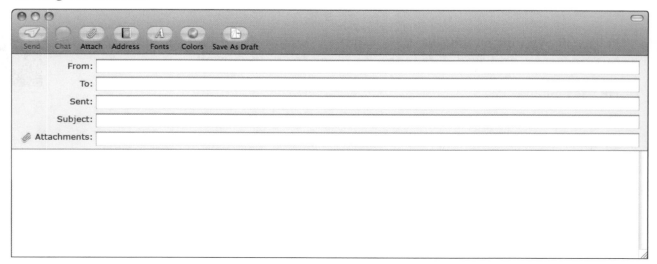

From:
To:
Sent:
Subject:
Attachments:

Speaking

13 Have a discussion with your partner on how to write an email with the help of 7Cs' principle (Conciseness, Completeness, Clearness, Consideration, Courtesy, Concreteness and Correctness).

Technical Terms

1 **Salutation** is the beginning of your email where you address the receiver, usually by name.

2 **Opening** is the first sentence in the email which refers to previous letter, contact or document.

3 **Body** is the main contents and messages of an email.

4 **Complimentary closing** is the word (such as "Sincerely") or phrase ("Best wishes") that come before the sender's signature and express the sender's regard for the receiver.

5 **Signature** is a block of text appended to the end of an email including the sender's name and contact information.

6 **Four Point Plan** is a simple framework for structuring of the content of an email, including introduction, details, conclusion and close.

   - **Introduction** includes the opening sentence, writing purpose and the background of the email.

   - **Details** refers to facts and figures, gives information and instructions, and provides all of the relevant details.

   - **Conclusion** refers to the response to the previous letter or the action will be taken.

   - **Close** is the last paragraph or sentence to express expectations.

Learning Objectives

Upon completion of the unit, students will be able to:

• understand the definition of marketing;

• design a marketing research questionnaire;

• identify the marketing mix.

Starting Off

In this unit you may be studying marketing in detail. But do you know what are the 4Ps and how to make the marketing strategy?

1 Put the specific marketing strategies A–P into the Marketing Mix of KFC.

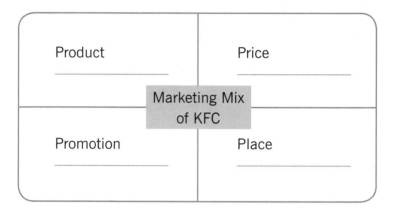

A KFC's outlets are located in downtown areas.

B KFC bundles different types of food together at a special rate.

C KFC uses all media like TV, hoardings, magazines, online ads etc.

D KFC is famous for its taglines like "Finger Lickin' Good", "Nobody Does Chicken like KFC" and "So Good".

E KFC's menu adjusts to regional tastes.

F Localisation strategy and public service activities of KFC will help in its brand building.

G Customers of KFC can order online and get their favorite chicken delivered to their doorstep.

H KFC offers Mexican Chicken Burrito and fried bread stick in China.

I The original product of KFC is pressure fried chicken nuggets flavored with secret seasoning of 11 ingredients.

J KFC has online and offline deliveries.

K KFC uses billboards and hoardings on city roads as well as highways.

L As KFC had association with Pepsi Co., most of the beverages served in KFC are from Pepsi.

M KFC sets price high and lowers the price by means of discount.

N KFC chooses the locations near the supermarkets, gasoline service stations.

O KFC gives discount to every new product. Also, online coupons are extremely high usage.

P KFC resets its price by different time, restaurants, and regions.

Reading **1**

Market Research

Today's business world is very **complex** but the basic **principle** is still this: companies make products they want to sell at a profit. What makes it complex is that consumers are becoming more and more **demanding**, and there is more and more competition with other companies which offer similar products so that consumers have a wide range of choice. Therefore companies must plan their activities very carefully: the way they market their products can mean the difference between them and competitors.

Marketing is the process of **identifying** and **satisfying** customers' needs. This process must be **satisfactory** for both sides: for the company because it must sell at a profit and for the consumer because he must be happy with the product so that he will buy it again. Marketing involves different activities. The first one **consists of** identifying the consumer's needs and wants, that is what the consumer needs and what he wants to buy. This activity **involves market research**, that is the process of collecting and **analysing** information about the market for a new or existing product. The objective of market research is to help the company identify the **target market**, that is the specific consumer group that will buy its product. A company needs to decide this before it starts to produce a product.

There are different methods of market research which can be used: **questionnaires**, telephone or personal interviews, **comments** on the Internet. They all consist of questions that give the company information about, for example:

- the customer's **profile**: his age, interests, lifestyle, etc.;
- the features of a product that customers want;
- the price they are willing to pay;
- the **features** of a product that they like or don't like;
- how often they use and buy a product.

MY GLOSSARY

complex	*adj.*	复杂的
principle	*n.*	原则; 原理
demanding	*adj.*	要求高的, 难满足的
marketing	*n.*	营销; 促销, 推销
identify	*v.*	发现; 确定, 辨别, 识别; 认出
satisfy	*v.*	使满意, 使满足; 使确信
satisfactory	*adj.*	令人满意的, 使人满足的
consist of		由……组成, 由……构成, 包含

involve	*v.*	涉及; 包括, 包含
market research		市场调查, 市场调研
analyse	*v.*	分析
target market		目标市场
questionnaire	*n.*	问卷; 情况调查表
comment	*n.*	评价, 评语, 评论; 意见
profile	*n.*	简介; 侧影; 传略; 影响力
feature	*n.*	特色, 特征; 面貌; 地形

2 Look at this list of steps and put them into the correct order.

☐ make the product

☐ distribute the product

☐ fix the price of the product at a profit

☐ advertise it

☐ understand what consumers need or want

3 Read the text and answer the questions below.

1) What is the final objective of any company?

_____

2) Why do consumers have a wide range of choice?

_____

3) What is the function of market research?

_____

4) How can a company carry out market research?

_____

5) What do these different methods consist of?

_____

6) What type of information can a company get with market research?

_____

4 Now read the text again and find definitions for the words and phrases below.

1) marketing: _____

2) market research: _____

3) target market: _____

5 Match the information to the question numbers from the questionnaire.

Royal Sport is a sportswear company. It is now planning to launch a new model of training shoes. This is the market research questionnaire they have prepared before they start design and production. What information does Royal Sport want?

1) Are you ☐ male or ☐ female?

2) How old are you?
☐ 15 – 20
☐ 21 – 30
☐ 31 – 40
☐ Over 40

3) How many trainers have you got?
☐ 1 pair
☐ 2 pairs
☐ 3 pairs
☐ More (please specify number) _____

4) How often do you buy a pair of trainers?
☐ Once a year
☐ Twice a year
☐ Three times a year
☐ More (please specify how often) _____

5) Are your trainers for a specific sport?
If yes, what sport?
☐ Yes ☐ No
☐ Tennis
☐ Football
☐ Jogging
☐ Basketball
☐ Other (please specify sport) _____

6) Where do you buy your trainers?
☐ Sports store
☐ Discount store
☐ The Internet
☐ Other (please specify place) _____

7) What are the features you look at, when buying your trainers?
☐ Design
☐ Price
☐ Brand name
☐ Comfort
☐ Popularity

8) How much are you willing to spend on your trainers? _____

9) Which is your favourite brand of trainers? _____

☐ **a** The average age of people who buy trainers

☐ **b** What influences their choice

☐ **c** If there are more men or more women interested in this article

☐ **d** The competitors

☐ **e** The place they usually go for their shopping

☐ **f** If they wear trainers every day or only when they do sport

☐ **g** If their potential customers buy many trainers

☐ **h** What consumers think is the right price

☐ **i** The frequency of buying trainers

Reading 2

The Marketing Mix

After selecting its target market with market research, a company must take decisions about the so called **marketing mix**, which is the **combination** of **Product**, Price, **Place** and **Promotion**. These four components help determine a clear and effective strategy to bring a product to market. This is the combination of 4Ps:

Product

Product refers to a good or service that a company offers to customers. This represents an item or service designed to satisfy customer needs and wants. It's important to identify what **differentiates** it from competing products or services.

Price

Setting a price is not easy. If the price is too high, consumers will not buy it. If it is too low, consumers will buy it but the money **earned** by the company may not be enough to **cover the costs**. Every company hopes to **make a profit**. This means that it must be sure that the price is higher than the cost of producing it. However, there are other factors to be considered. For example, it may be useful to see what competitors do: if they offer similar products, their price can be a good **starting point**. Also, if a company has used market research to ask **potential customers** what price they are willing to pay for its product, this is another important factor. After setting a product's price, a company may decide to **offer** discounts which means offering reduced prices to customers who buy large quantities of a product, who pay cash, who buy a product **out of season** or at the end of a season, that is during **sales**.

Place

Place refers to the **distribution** of a product, that is the process of getting a product from the producer to the consumer. Between the producer and the consumer there are **intermediaries** like **wholesalers**, who buy from producers and sell to **retailers**, and retailers who buy from wholesalers and sell to consumers. The majority of consumers buy from retailers, but there are different types of retailers.

Promotion

Promotion is the **element** of the 4Ps that people **associate** most with marketing. It is a form of **persuasive** communication that **motivates** consumers to buy a product. The most popular methods of promotion areadvertising and **sales promotions**.

Internet Marketing

Internet marketing or i-marketing has **dramatically** changed the marketing world. Its ability to identify and target markets at a **fraction** of what it once cost has made it the ideal tool for any business, be it the largest **multinational** or a start-up fashion designer selling T-shirts from a **basement**.

I-marketing can be used to **conduct** market research and to promote products and/or services **in addition to**, or as a **replacement** of, more traditional methods.

Large companies are now using **social media** like **Twitter** and **Facebook** as an **extension** of their market research department, while small companies rely entirely on these sources to find out what a market wants and what people are willing to pay for a new product or service. Studying Twitter **chatter** and following Facebook comments have become the new focus groups and consumer **panels**. When you use a company **app** or the "Like" **button** on a Facebook page, you are willingly and knowingly sharing your information with third parties. However many internet users are unaware of how much information companies are gathering about us, our habits, lifestyles, likes and dislikes every time we use a **search engine**, visit a website or **click** on a **link**. **Cookies**, **tracking codes** and **databases** are all ways in which a company can track and store our personal information for later use.

Thanks to these **tracking devices**, internet ads promoting products and services can be **targeted** to a specific **audience**, increasing their chance of success. To reach a wider audience and improve its **internet presence**, a company can use **SEO**, while a company **blog** will help in promoting a **corporate image**.

MY GLOSSARY

marketing mix		营销组合	associate	v.	联系, 关联
combination	n.	组合; 联合	persuasive	adj.	有说服力的; 劝诱的, 劝说的
product	n.	产品			
place	n.	营销渠道; 地点; 位置	motivate	v.	激发……的积极性; 刺激; 使有动机
promotion	n.	促销			
differentiate	v.	区分, 区别	sales promotion		促销
set a price		定价	internet marketing		网络营销
earn	v.	挣钱; 挣得, 赢得	dramatically	adv.	显著地, 剧烈地; 戏剧地
cover the cost		足够支付成本	fraction	n.	小部分; 稍微; 分数
make a profit		盈利, 获利	multinational	n.	跨国公司
starting point		起点	basement	n.	地下室, 地窖
potential customer		潜在客户	conduct	v.	实施; 进行
offer	v.	提供; 报价	in addition to		除……之外
out of season		过季的(水果和蔬菜)	replacement	n.	替代, 更换; 复位; 代替者
sales	n.	促销, 打折	social media		社会媒体
distribution	n.	营销渠道; 分布, 分配	Twitter	n.	推特
intermediary	n.	中间人, 仲裁者, 调解者; 媒介物	Facebook	n.	脸书
wholesaler	n.	批发商	extension	n.	拓展, 延伸
retailor	n.	零售商	chatter	n.	聊天; 唠叨; 饶舌
element	n.	要素, 成分; 原理	panel	n.	小组; 仪表板; 嵌板
			app (application)	abbr.	(计算机)应用程序

button	n.	按钮; 纽扣	target	v.	面向, 对准（某群体）; 把……作为目标
search engine		搜索引擎	audience	n.	观众, 听众, 读者
click	v.	点击	internet presence		网上曝光
link	n.	链接; 环节	SEO	abbr.	搜索引擎优化（search engine optimisation）
cookies	n.	信息记录程序			
tracking code		跟踪代码	blog	n.	博客, 部落格; 网络日志
database	n.	数据库	corporate image		企业形象, 公司形象
tracking device		跟踪设备			

6 Match the 4Ps in column II to their definitions in column I. And then match the 4Ps in column II to what exactly the 4Ps involve in column III.

I	II	III
a the distribution of the product	☐1☐ Product	A involves the money spent by the consumer plus the profit for the company
b the method to persuade consumers to buy the product	☐2☐ Price	B involves how and where consumers can buy the product
c the type of goods to produce	☐3☐ Promotion	C involves giving the product a name, an image, a design, a packaging, a quality
d the cost of the product to the buyer	☐4☐ Place	D involves deciding how to make consumers know about the product and persuade

7 Match column I to column II.

I	II
Read the paragraph about Price and match the first part of the sentence to the second part.	
☐1) Setting a price is not easy because	A be sure that the price is higher than the cost of producing it; see what competitors do; see what price potential customers are willing to pay for the product.
☐2) The three factors to consider when setting a price are	B buy large quantities of a product, who pay cash, who buy a product out of season or at the end of a season, that is during sales.
☐3) A discount is a	C if the price is too high, consumers will not buy the product. If it is too low, consumers will buy it but the money earned by the company may not be enough to cover the costs.
☐4) Discounts can be offered to customers who	D reduced price for customers

I	II
Read the paragraph about Place and match the names of different stores in column I to their definitions in column II.	
☐ 5) department store	**E** store that sells one type of article from different manufacturers at regular prices
☐ 6) shopping centre/Mall	**F** large store with different departments for different articles
☐ 7) factory outlet	**G** websites where consumers buy directly
☐ 8) specialty store	**H** many different shops in the same place
☐ 9) discount store	**I** mall with stores that sell designer articles at low prices
☐ 10) internet	**J** store that sells brand name articles at discounted prices
☐ 11) outlet	**K** store that sells articles from a specific manufacturer at discounted prices
Read the paragraph about Promotion. Look at these examples of sales promotions in column I and match them to the definitions in column II.	
☐ 12) free gifts (or freebies)	**L** certificates that offer discounts on particular products and can be found in newspapers or on the product
☐ 13) samples	**M** cards given by stores or supermarkets that give advantages to owners: building up points to get gifts from a catalogue or discounts
☐ 14) coupons	**N** extra objects included with a product at no extra cost
☐ 15) buy one, get one free offers	**O** small sized version of a product offered free
☐ 16) loyalty cards	**P** an offer of getting 2 products for the price of one
Read the paragraph about Promotion and match the types of promotion in column I to the pictures in column II.	
☐ 17) free gifts (or freebies)	**Q**
☐ 18) samples	**R**
☐ 19) coupons	**S**
☐ 20) buy one, get one free offers	**T**
☐ 21) loyalty cards	**U**

8 **Read the paragraphs about Internet Marketing and decide if the sentences are true (_T_) or false (_F_). If there is not enough information, choose "doesn't say" (_DS_).**

	T	F	DS
1) I-marketing costs much more than traditional marketing.	☐	☐	☐
2) It is only useful for large multinationals.	☐	☐	☐
3) Social networks have been advantageous for i-marketing.	☐	☐	☐
4) Analysing what people say on social networks is a way of collecting data.	☐	☐	☐
5) All internet users know about tracking devices used to obtain personal information.	☐	☐	☐
6) Cookies are the most common way of tracking internet users.	☐	☐	☐
7) Companies use the information collected by tracking devices to target their advertising.	☐	☐	☐
8) SEO should only be used by companies with high traffic to their website.	☐	☐	☐

9 **Read the paragraphs about Internet Marketing and find the verbs in the text for the definitions.**

1) to recognise or distinguish something   ....

2) to select as an object of attention   ....

3) to organise and carry out   ....

4) to learn or discover a fact   ....

5) to collect, group together from different places   ....

6) to follow the trail or movements of someone or something   ....

7) to keep or accumulate something for future use   ....

Listening

10 **John Newman works in the Research and Development Department of a company that produces make-up products for teenagers. Listen to him speaking about the importance of packaging in marketing and choose the right options.**

1) If a company wants to sell a successful product, it has to

   A. sell it at a competitive price.

   B. differentiate it from competitors.

2) plays an essential role in marketing strategy.

   A. Packaging

   B. Advertising

3) What attracts a consumer at first is

   A. the look of a product.

   B. the marketing strategy chosen by a company.

4) Packaging… a container for a product.

   A. is simply

   B. is not simply

5) Packaging helps to

   A. protect a product and identify a brand.

   B. identify a product and sell a product.

11 **Listen to Ann Moore, a marketing consultant, talking about advertising and complete the text.**

To start with, I'd like to give a definition of (1) _____ and to specify its objectives.

Advertising is the process of communicating (2) _____ about a product and of persuading people to (3) _____ it. There are different advertising media with advantages and disadvantages. Let's start with (4) _____ which has a great impact on consumers. TV adverts can be shown several times a day but people can decide not to watch them. Then, (5) _____ or magazines. It is true that they both reach a large number of (6) _____ but the limit is that they are static, so they may have less impact than TV adverts because they don't attract consumers' attention so much. Billboards and (7) _____ displayed outdoors can be effective only if they are (8) _____ but people may not notice them. Finally the (9) _____, of course advertising over the Internet is the way to reach the largest number of consumers and it has a "total" impact: sight, sound and motion. But consumers may ignore it and (10) _____ it off.

Writing

12 Choose a popular product you know for each of the product categories in the table below. Then, try to identify the possible consumer profile for each product, including the information required. And then, write your results following the guidelines.

Category	Product	Consumer Profile
Rucksack		Age: Sex: Competitors: Price:
Watch		Age: Sex: Competitors: Price:
Car		Age: Sex: Competitors: Price:
PC		Age: Sex: Competitors: Price:

The product I have analysed is _____.

In my opinion, the typical consumer is about (age) _____, and usually male/female.

He/She would find similar products among these brands: _____.

Finally, he/she would be willing to pay about _____ euros for this product.

Speaking

13 Discuss the questions in small groups.

1) Do you think i-marketing has positive or negative effects for consumers? For companies?

2) Will it replace other market research methods?

3) Do you think it is correct that your internet movements can be tracked? Why/Why not?

Technical Terms

1 **Questionnaire** is a list of questions that people are asked so that information can be collected about something.

2 **Target market** is the group of people that a company wants to sell its products or services to.

3 **Marketing** refers to activities a company undertakes to promote the buying or selling of a product or service.

4 **Marketing strategy** refers to a business's overall game plan for reaching prospective consumers and turning them into customers of the products or services.

5 **Marketing mix** refers to the set of actions, or tactics, that a company uses to promote its brand or product in the market. The 4Ps make up a typical marketing mix — Price, Product, Promotion and Place.

6 **Price** refers to pricing the products or the services according to the costs, segment targeted, ability of the market to pay, supply-demand and factors in order to differentiate and enhance the image of a product.

7 **Product** refers to the various of products or services being sold in order to meet the different demands of the consumers.

8 **Place** refers to the different distribution channels of selling products or providing services.

9 **Promotion** refers to all the activities undertaken in order to make the product or service known to the user and trade, which include advertising, word of mouth, press reports, incentives, commissions, awards to the trade, consumer schemes, direct marketing, contests, prizes and public relations.

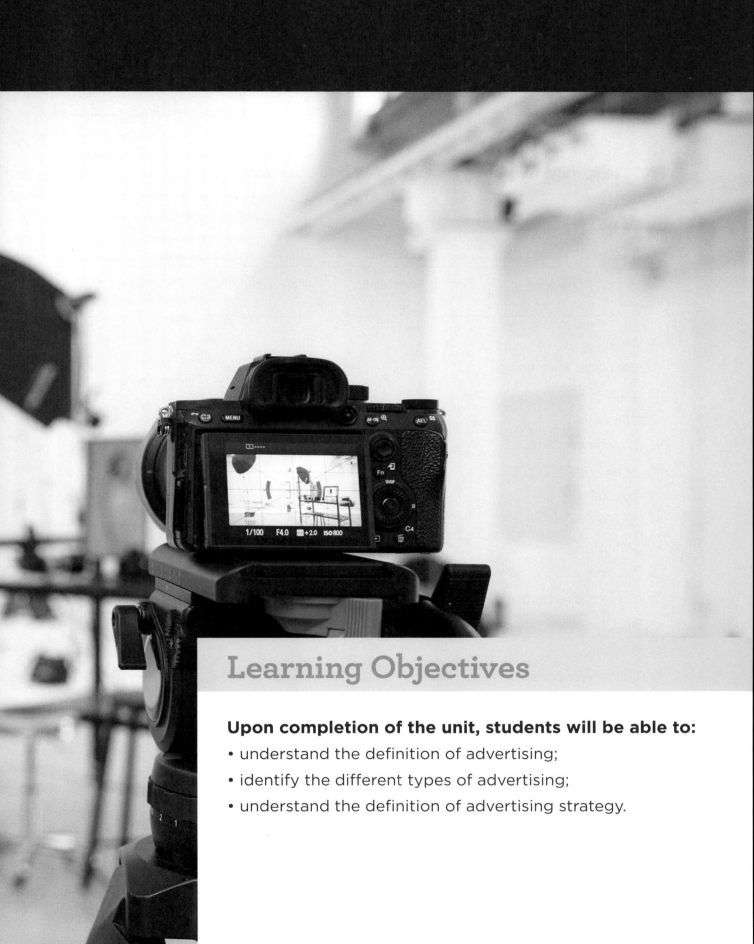

Learning Objectives

Upon completion of the unit, students will be able to:

- understand the definition of advertising;
- identify the different types of advertising;
- understand the definition of advertising strategy.

In this unit you may be studying advertising in detail. But do you know the different kinds of advertising?

1 **Put the specific marketing strategies A–S into the chart.**

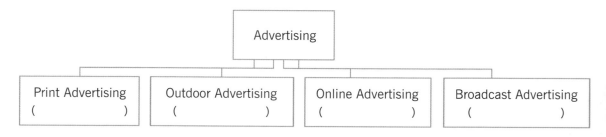

Advertising

| Print Advertising ( ) | Outdoor Advertising ( ) | Online Advertising ( ) | Broadcast Advertising ( ) |

A radio

B periodical advertising

C website

D magazine

E social media site

F newspaper

G big board

H brochure

I leaflet

J handout

K direct mail advertising

L app

M billboard

N bus shelter poster

O BBS

P poster

Q neon sign

R television

S commercials

Reading 1

The Purpose of Advertising

Advertising is perhaps the most important **aspect** of promotion, the fourth P in the marketing mix, and is used to **persuade**, **inform** and **remind**. It can persuade consumers to buy or use an existing product or service; it can inform them about changes within a company or a new product or service; it can remind them about a company, thus improving its image and building **brand identity**. Companies generally **divide** their advertising into two **distinct** areas:

- **Business-to-consumer (B2C) advertising**: to persuade the **general public** to buy the company's products or use its services.

- **Business-to-business (B2B) advertising**: **directed** at other businesses to inform them about the company and to promote its products and services.

The first thing an advertisement has to do is to **grab** our attention and it can achieve this in a variety of ways: a **slogan**, a **striking** image, a **catchy jingle** or a **memorable headline**. The second thing is to provide more information about the product or service. In a **print ad**, this will be the body of the ad. The purpose is to create feelings of belief, trust and desire. The third aspect is to make sure that potential customers can remember the company or product and to **reinforce** the brand identity, for example with the logo. The final element, the **call to action**, may be **implicit** within the ad or specified **explicitly**, such as inviting **viewers** to click on a website or visit a store. Since we are surrounded by advertising **in all aspects** of our lives, we are perhaps becoming more **resistant** and less open to advertising. Therefore agencies and ad designers have to try to make their ad **stand out in a crowd** and new **advertising models** are continuously developed and new media **options explored** so as to continue to reach the **target audience**.

Effective Advertising

When creating an advert and defining an advertising campaign, most businesses use the services of an **advertising agency**. Here **specialists** follow all aspects from the definition of the **USP (Unique Selling Proposition)** and the creation of the ad, to the selection of the advertising media and the **length** and **timing** of the campaign.

When creating an ad, agencies and ad designers can try to achieve the objectives of a successful advert—that it should be noticed, read, believed, remembered and **acted upon**—in different ways. They can use a traditional approach or try to be more **original**. Both of these have advantages as well as potential **drawbacks**. Traditional language, images and **associations** have been tried and tested and are known to work. On the other hand, **random** or unconnected images, **bizarre** headlines or **invented** words can be considered **groundbreaking** and modern. The **downsides** are that the first approach may just seem boring and over-used; the second could be too **obscure** to be properly understood or to **catch on**.

Humour is another common technique and it is often considered the most successful by consumers and agencies alike, as a funny or **entertaining** ad is more likely to be remembered.

The use of famous people as **testimonials** can also be considered. A famous actor, sportsperson or model has a very powerful personal image and can bring this to the advert. However, it can be an extremely expensive option and public opinion about who is **"in" or cool** can change very fast. **Gossip** and **scandals** surrounding a **celebrity** also **risk** damaging the company's image.

MY GLOSSARY

aspect	n.	方面; 方向; 形势; 外貌
persuade	v.	说服
inform	v.	通知; 告诉; 报告
remind	v.	提醒
brand identity		品牌标识; 品牌认可度
divide	v.	分成, 分开
distinct	adj.	不同的; 明显的; 独特的
business-to-consumer (B2C) advertising		企业对消费者的广告
general public		公众
business-to-business (B2B) advertising		企业对企业的广告
direct	v.	面向……; 指导; 指挥; 管理
grab	v.	抓住; 攫取, 夺取
slogan	n.	标语
striking	adj.	引人注目的, 显著的, 突出的
catchy	adj.	悦耳易记的; 引人注意的
jingle	n.	简单而又引人注意的韵律
memorable headline		难忘的标题
print ad	n.	印刷广告; 平面广告
reinforce	v.	加强, 加固, 强化
call to action		唤起行动, 行动号召
implicit	adj.	暗示的, 含蓄的; 盲从的

explicitly	adv.	明确地
viewer	n.	观众
in all aspects		在各个方面
resistant	adj.	抵抗的, 反抗的
stand out in a crowd		鹤立鸡群
advertising model		广告模式
option	n.	选项; 选择权
explore	v.	探索; 探测
target audience		目标客户
advertising agency		广告公司, 广告商
specialist	n.	专家; 专门医师
USP (Unique Selling Proposition)		独特卖点
length	n.	长度
timing	n.	时间选择; 调速; 定时
act upon		对……起作用; 按照……行事
original	adj.	新颖的; 原创的
drawback	n.	缺点; 不利条件
association	n.	联想; 联合; 协会; 联盟
random	adj.	任意的, 随机的
bizarre	adj.	奇异的, 匪夷所思的
invented	adj.	发明创造的
groundbreaking	adj.	开创性的
downside	n.	缺点, 负面; 下降趋势; 底侧

obscure	adj.	晦涩的; 不清楚的, 朦胧的	"in" or cool		时髦或者酷
catch on		变得流行; 理解, 明白	gossip	n.	小道消息, 八卦闲话
humour	n.	幽默	scandal	n.	丑闻; 流言蜚语
entertaining	adj.	令人愉快的	celebrity	n.	名人; 名声
testimonial	n.	推荐; 证明	risk	v.	冒险

2 Read the text and answer the questions.

1) What is the purpose of advertising?

2) What is the difference between B2B and B2C advertising?

3) What are the five things that an advert should do?

4) How can an advert catch our attention?

5) How does an advert try to make us remember a product or company?

6) Do you believe that consumers today are more resistant to advertising? Why/Why not?

3 Match each element of an advert on the left to the correct definition on the right.

1) slogan   a ☐ the photograph, pictures or other visual elements in an advert

2) image   b ☐ the main text of a print ad, with information on the product or service

3) jingle   c ☐ a short, well thought-out sentence, usually the first part of a print ad to be read

4) headline   d ☐ the unique symbol used by a company or brand

5) body   e ☐ a memorable tune or piece of music, mostly used in radio commercials

6) logo   f ☐ a short, catchy and distinctive phrase to describe a product or a brand

4 Read the text and decide if the sentences are true (*T*) or false (*F*). If there is not enough information, choose "doesn't say" (*DS*).

	T	F	DS
1) Advertising agencies only follow big clients.	☐	☐	☐
2) Advertising agencies' services are limited to the creative aspect of an ad.	☐	☐	☐
3) A traditional approach to creating an ad does not have any disadvantages.	☐	☐	☐
4) An original ad may contain strange or made-up words.	☐	☐	☐
5) Both consumers and agencies believe humorous ads to be successful.	☐	☐	☐
6) The use of famous people in ad campaigns is in decline.	☐	☐	☐

5 Translate the following sentences into Chinese.

1) Both of these have advantages as well as potential drawbacks. Traditional language, images and associations have been tried and tested and are known to work. On the other hand, random or unconnected images, bizarre headlines or invented words can be considered groundbreaking and modern. The downsides are that the first approach may just seem boring and over-used; the second could be too obscure to be properly understood or to catch on.

_____

_____

_____

2) The use of famous people as testimonials can also be considered. A famous actor, sportsperson or model has a very powerful personal image and can bring this to the advert. However, it can be an extremely expensive option and public opinion about who is "in" or cool can change very fast. Gossip and scandals surrounding a celebrity also risk damaging the company's image.

_____

_____

_____

_____

Reading 2

Advertising Media

The choice of the media for an advertising campaign depends on several factors, including:
- size, nature and location of the target market;
- the product or service to be promoted;
- what **proportion** of the target audience will be **exposed** to the ad;
- the cost.

TV

This is still the most popular choice given its high **impact** and **wide national reach**. It is **effective** for creating **brand awareness** and selling consumer products. However, with the large number of **satellite** and **cable TV channels** now available, it is no longer **sufficient** to advertise just on the top three or four networks, but it is essential to choose the channel and **programme** with the specific **demographic** required. TV advertising is **extremely** expensive, especially for the **prime time slots** such as early evening or during sporting events, and similarly the **investment** needed to produce the ad itself is huge. Another downside of TV advertising is that new **digital technology** allows viewers to **skip** adverts during **playback** or **viewing**, or viewers may just take a break or **channel hop** during the **commercial breaks**.

Press

The **press** has a **leading role** in advertising campaigns. Printed adverts have the advantage that they can be kept, are often seen repeatedly and can contain more information or details than a TV ad. Their visual impact is still great even without sound or movement. Depending on the target, in an ad campaign it is possible to include international, national and regional newspapers (often a **specific section** like business, sport or fashion) and general interest or special interest magazines (e.g. computer, sport, hobbies). Naturally, a full colour ad in a **glossy magazine** is more expensive, and reaches a larger audience, than a black and white ad at the back of a local newspaper.

Radio

Radio is a cheaper **alternative** to TV advertising, both to purchase the airtime and to make the ad. It can be national or local but does not reach the same number of people as TV. The creation of the ad has to be carefully considered as it cannot rely on the impact of **visual images**.

Outdoor

Outdoor advertising includes **billboards**, **posters**, **street furniture** and **electric signs** in public places such as the street, shopping centres, airports, stations and on public transport. Some are much more **permanent** and have become almost part of the background, while others are changed more frequently, such as on public transport, to maintain impact. The target is the general public, although the **location**, for example in a football **stadium** or near a school, can target a more specific market segment.

Digital Media

The most rapidly growing **sector**, **digital media**, especially internet, offers targeted advertising worldwide 24/7 with **banners**, **pop up ads**, and pay per click advertising, as well as one-to-one emails. Digital advertising is inexpensive, can use sound, visuals and **motion** to create impact and it is easy to **update** and **evaluate** the **success rate**. A disadvantage is that these ads are very easy for users to ignore while **surfing** and to **delete** from their **inbox**. With social media and apps, advertisers are able to form a more direct contact with consumers, especially young people, creating a **global community** around a brand or product with **consequent** positive effects on sales and brand identity. Another advantage of social media is how **swiftly** messages can be spread. **Viral ads**, for example, can be posted on YouTube or Facebook where they are noticed by net surfers and shared immediately, quickly reaching millions of **hits**.

satellite	n.	卫星, 人造卫星	
cable TV channel		有线电视频道	
sufficient	adj.	足够的; 充分的	
programme	n.	电视节目; 计划; 程序	
demographic	n.	特定年龄段的人口	
extremely	adv.	非常, 极其; 极端地	
prime time slot		黄金时段	
investment	n.	投资; 投入	
digital technology		数字技术	
skip	v.	跳过, 遗漏	
playback	n.	重放; 录音	
viewing	n.	收看(电视); 察看, 观看	
channel hop		更换频道	
commercial break		（广播、电视中插播的）商业广告	
press	n.	报刊杂志; 新闻界; 出版社	
leading role		主导作用; 主导地位	
specific section		特定的部分	
glossy magazine		用优质有光纸印刷的杂志	
radio	n.	无线电广播; 收音机	
alternative	n.	供替代的选择	
airtime	n.	（广播或电视）播放时间	
visual image		视觉影像	
outdoor	adj.	户外的, 露天的	

billboard	n.	广告牌, 户外看板
poster	n.	海报; 广告
street furniture		街道公共设施
electric sign		广告灯牌, 电子标牌
permanent	adj.	长久的; 不变的, 永久的
location	n.	位置, 地点
stadium	n.	体育场
sector	n.	部分; 区域; 部门
digital media		数字媒体
banner	n.	横幅图片的广告模式; 横幅, 标语
pop up ad		弹出广告
motion	n.	动作; 移动
update	v.	更新; （使）现代化
evaluate	v.	评价; 估价
success rate		成功率; 接通率
surf	v.	上网; 冲浪
delete	v.	删除
inbox	n.	收件箱
global community		全球社区; 地球村
consequent	adj.	随之发生的; 作为结果的
swiftly	adv.	迅捷地; 即刻
viral ad		病毒式广告
hit	n.	网页点击数

6 **Match the advertising media in column I to the picture in column II.**

I	II
1) press	A 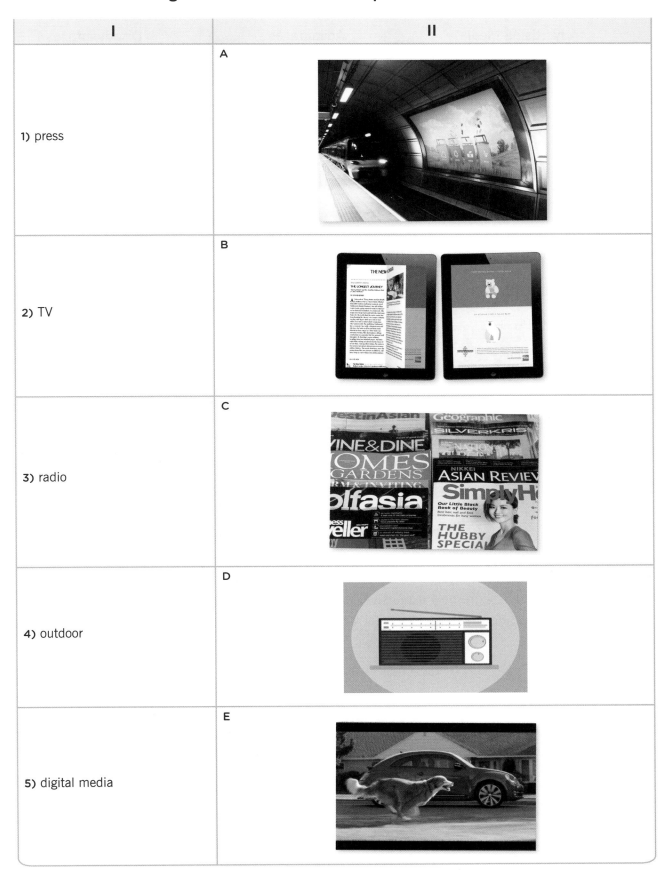
2) TV	B
3) radio	C
4) outdoor	D
5) digital media	E

7 **Read the text again and complete this table.**

Advertising Media	Advantages	Disadvantages
1) press		
2) TV		
3) radio		
4) outdoor		
5) digital media		

8 **Which advertising media do the terms refer to? Write a definition for each term.**

1) prime time slot _____

2) channel hopping _____

3) glossy magazine _____

4) trade press _____

5) billboard _____

6) street furniture _____

7) banner _____

8) pop up ad _____

9 **Translate the following sentences into Chinese.**

1) TV advertising is extremely expensive, especially for the prime time slots such as early evening or during sporting events, and similarly the investment needed to produce the ad itself is huge.

_____

_____

2) The most rapidly growing sector, digital media, especially internet, offers targeted advertising worldwide 24/7 with banners, pop up ads, and pay per click advertising, as well as one-to-one emails.

_____

_____

Listening

10 **Listen to the passage and complete the following sentences.**

1) A shampoo available in supermarkets _____ .

2) A local repair service for electrical appliances _____ .

3) A website selling children's toys _____ .

4) A low-cost dental surgery in your town _____ .

5) A cruise holidays in the Caribbean _____ .

6) An energy drink _____ .

11 **Listen to this manager from an advertising agency talking about creating an effective ad and complete the notes.**

Step 1 – have a clear _____ so your message is focused.

Step 2 – understand the _____ of your ad to make it appropriate and produce results.

Step 3 – show how your product or service will _____ a consumer.

Step 4 – know your USP to define your _____ and use it in your advert.

Step 5 – _____ with the customer, be motivating and encouraging but always believable.

Writing

12 Write a rental ad for an office according to the following instruction.

> Product offered: Office (2000 square feet)
> Words to persuade: new, convenient
> Detailed information given: downtown, one block away from subway station
> Contact: Mr White (Tel: 136-6840-3967)

Speaking

13 Discuss the questions in pairs.

1) Were the ads you remembered more traditional or innovative? In what ways?

2) Did the ads use any humour? If so, do you think it was entertaining or funny?

3) Did the ads feature a famous person? Who? What ideas do you associate with him/her?

4) In general, which of the above-mentioned techniques do you prefer in an ad? Why?

Technical Terms

1 **Advertising** is the business of trying to persuade people to buy products or services.

2 **Advertisement** is a picture, short film, song, etc. that tries to persuade people to buy a product or service, or a piece of text that tells people about the product or service, etc.

3 **Advertising strategy** is a detailed plan developed by businesses to create awareness among the customers about the product or service and motivate the customers to buy them.

4 **Online advertising** is the advertisement shown via the Internet or through mobile devices.

5 **Print advertising** is the advertisement on printed pieces, such as newspapers or magazines.

6 **Broadcast advertising** is the advertisement performed on video or audio mass media such as television and radio.

7 **Outdoor advertising**, also known as out-of-home (OOH) advertising, is any type of advertising that reaches consumers when they are away from home, such as billboards beside the road, or at sports games, etc.

Learning Objectives

Upon completion of the unit, students will be able to:

• draw the flow chart of business transaction;

• make an enquiry;

• reply an enquiry.

Starting Off

In this unit you may be studying business transaction. But do you know the normative symbols of Transaction Flow Chart?

1 **Match the normative symbols in column I to the application descriptions in column II and the graphs in column III.**

I	II	III
☐☐ **1)** The Rectangle Shape	**A** represents the start/end.	a
☐☐ **2)** The Diamond Shape	**B** represents a process.	b
☐☐ **3)** The Oval or Pill Shape	**C** represents the input/output of the information.	c
☐☐ **4)** The Parallelogram Shape	**D** represents a decision.	d
☐☐ **5)** The Arrow Shape	**E** represents the flow of the sequence.	e

Reading 1

Business Transaction

Business involves buying and selling goods or services. When a buyer buys from a seller (and a seller sells to a buyer), this is called a **business transaction**. There are different steps in a business transaction including enquiry, reply to enquiry, **order** and reply to the order.

Enquiry

```
                                            1
Send   Chat   Attach  Address  Fonts  Colors  Save As Draft

   From:  areynolds@futuresport.uk
     To:  george.altmann@bestonsportstuff.com
   Sent:  Friday 24/01/2020 18:46
Subject:  enquiry
Attachments:
```

Dear Mr Altmann,

I'm writing to ask if you produce **Art. No.** 74 of your catalogue in yellow. If yes, I'd like to know what discount you can give us for an order of 200 **items**.
Can you also let us know when you can **deliver** them?
I look forward to your reply.

Best regards,
Anthony Reynolds

Reply to Enquiry

```
                                            2
Send   Chat   Attach  Address  Fonts  Colors  Save As Draft

   From:  george.altmann@bestonsportstuff.com
     To:  areynolds@futuresport.uk
   Sent:  Monday 27/01/2020 09:05
Subject:  your enquiry
Attachments:  catalogue
```

Dear Mr Reynolds,

Many thanks for your email. I attach a copy of our catalogue showing Art. No. 74 in yellow and other colours.
For an order of 200 items, we can give you a 5% discount.
We can **guarantee** delivery in about 2 weeks from **receipt** of order.
Hope to hear from you soon.

Regards
George Altmann

business transaction		商务贸易
order	n.	订单; 订购
Art. No. (Article Number)	abbr.	货号
item	n.	商品

deliver	v.	交货; 交付; 递送, 运输
guarantee	v.	保证; 保修
receipt	n.	收到; 收据; 收入

2 Look at this flow chart showing the 4 basic steps and match them with the corresponding explanation.

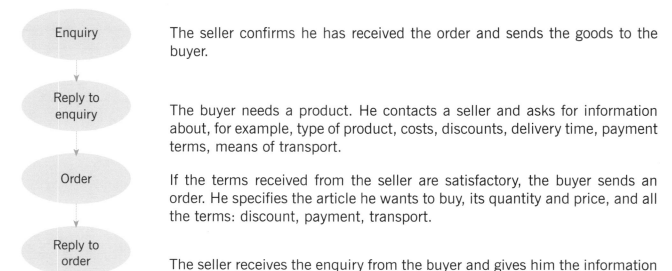

Enquiry

The seller confirms he has received the order and sends the goods to the buyer.

Reply to enquiry

The buyer needs a product. He contacts a seller and asks for information about, for example, type of product, costs, discounts, delivery time, payment terms, means of transport.

Order

If the terms received from the seller are satisfactory, the buyer sends an order. He specifies the article he wants to buy, its quantity and price, and all the terms: discount, payment, transport.

Reply to order

The seller receives the enquiry from the buyer and gives him the information requested.

3 The words and expressions below are frequently used in the emails. Write the corresponding words in Chinese.

1) item a _____

2) discount b _____

3) deliver c _____

4) hear from you d _____

5) look forward to e _____

6) (best) regards f _____

7) attach g _____

8) catalogue h _____

9) receipt i _____

10) dear j _____

4 **Read the emails and complete the table.**

	The Buyer	The Seller
Product	He wants to know if	He replies that they do and
Discount	He asks what	He replies that
Delivery	He asks when	He replies that

5 **Translate the two emails in the text into Chinese.**

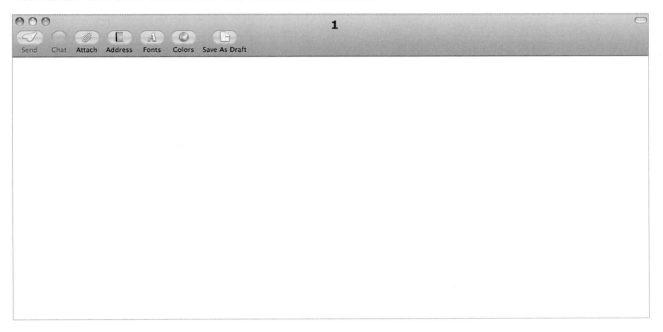

Reading 2

Business Transaction

Business involves buying and selling goods or services. When a buyer buys from a seller (and a seller sells to a buyer), this is called a business transaction. There are different steps in a business transaction including enquiry, reply to enquiry, order and reply to the order.

Order

From: areynolds@futuresport.uk
To: george.altmann@bestonsportstuff.com
Sent: Tuesday 11/02/2020 10:13
Subject: order
Attachments:

Dear Mr Altmann,

We would like to pass you the following order:

Art.No	Description	Quantity	Unit Price	Total Price
74	yellow sport bag	200	£58.60	£11,720.00
			5% discount £586.00	
			TOTAL £11,134.00	

Delivery by 26 February is **essential**.

We will **effect payment** 30 days from invoice date, as usual.

We **look forward to** your reply.

Regards,
Anthony Reynolds

Reply to the Order

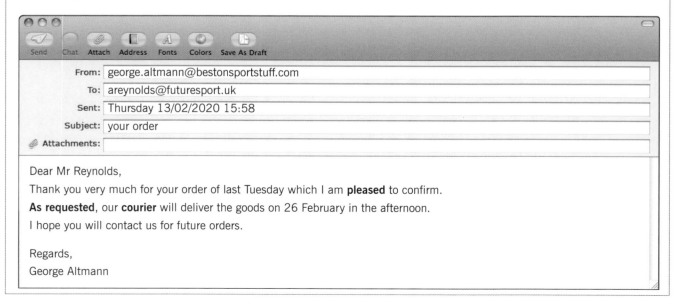

From: george.altmann@bestonsportstuff.com
To: areynolds@futuresport.uk
Sent: Thursday 13/02/2020 15:58
Subject: your order
Attachments:

Dear Mr Reynolds,

Thank you very much for your order of last Tuesday which I am **pleased** to confirm.

As requested, our **courier** will deliver the goods on 26 February in the afternoon.

I hope you will contact us for future orders.

Regards,
George Altmann

MY GLOSSARY

description	*n.*	规格; 描述, 描写	
unit price		单价	
total price		总价	
essential	*adj.*	重要的; 基本的; 本质的	
effect payment		支付款项	

look forward to		期待	
pleased	*adj.*	乐意的, 高兴的, 喜欢的	
as requested		按照要求, 依照要求, 应……要求	
courier	*n.*	货运公司; 邮递员	

6 **After receiving the reply from Beston Sportstuff, Anthony Reynolds from Future Sport sends the order in Reading 2. Read it and find this information.**

1) How many items he orders: _____

2) What type of articles he orders: _____

3) How much each item costs: _____

4) How much he will pay in total: _____

5) When he wants to receive the goods: _____

6) How he will pay: _____

7 **Read Beston Sportstuff's reply in Reading 2 and circle Yes or No to the questions.**

1) Does Mr Altmann confirm receipt of the order from Future Sport? Yes / No

2) Will the goods be delivered when the client wants? Yes / No

8 Translate the two emails in the text into Chinese.

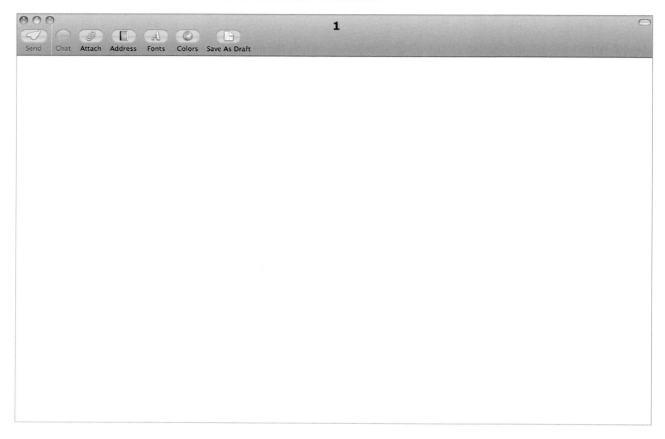

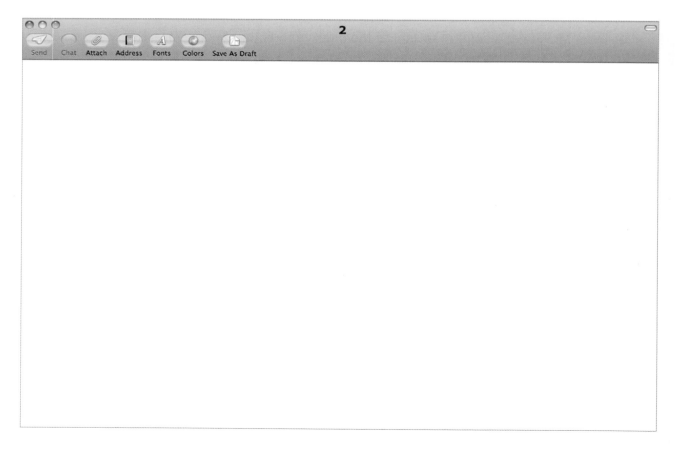

9 Complete this enquiry and reply emails using words and phrases from the emails in this unit.

The enquiry

(1) _____ Mrs Smart,

I (2) _____ to ask if you can send us your best price for your mobile phone covers, Art. No. AA64 of your catalogue.
(3) _____ also let us know about possible discounts, delivery times and means of payment requested?
We look (4) _____ .

Best (5) _____ ,
David Hobbs

The reply

Dear (6) _____ ,

Many (7) _____ your enquiry about our mobile phone covers. I (8) _____ a copy of our catalogue with information about the article. For an order of about 100 items, we can (9) _____ 10% (10) _____ .
We (11) _____ delivery (12) _____ 1 month from (13) _____ .
We require (14) _____ 30 days from (15) _____ .
We look (16) _____ your order.

(17) _____ ,
Margaret Smart

Listening

10 Listen to 8 sentences taken from 8 dialogues and write which steps of a business transactions they refer to.

1)	
2)	
3)	
4)	
5)	
6)	
7)	
8)	

Enquiry

↓

Reply to enquiry

↓

Order

↓

Reply to order

11 David Hobbs decides to send an order to Margaret Smart. Listen to him talking about the order with his secretary and complete the order form they will send to their supplier.

Order Form
Contact: David Hobbs

Art. No	Colour	Quantity	Unit Price

Delivery: _____

Payment: _____

Writing

12 Write the reply to David Hobbs' order from Margaret Smart in Exercise 11 following the guidelines below.

— thank him for his order and confirm it

— say that delivery will be effected as requested

— say you hope he will contact you for future orders

Speaking

13 Suppose you and your partner are the buyer and the seller. Make a bargain by phone including the following information.

— the delivery date

— discount allowed

— methods of payment

Technical Terms

1 **Offer** is a conditional proposal made by a buyer or seller to buy or sell some kinds of goods or services, which becomes legally binding if accepted.

2 **Offeror** is the party making the offer, who is willing to sell or buy some kinds of good or services at a price.

3 **Offeree** is the other party to the agreement, who has the right to accept or refuse the offer.

4 **Acceptance** is the final agreement of both parties to consent to the terms of the offer.

5 **Counteroffer** is a response given to an initial offer which means the original offer was rejected and replaced with another one.

6 **Rejection** is the process of refusing an offer or terminating an offer.

8 Placing Orders

Learning Objectives

Upon completion of the unit, students will be able to:

• place an order;

• accept an order;

• refuse an order.

Starting Off

In this unit you may be studying orders. But do you know how to place an order on the Walmart app or website?

1 **Put the following steps into the correct order to show how to place your order on Walmart website[1] below.**

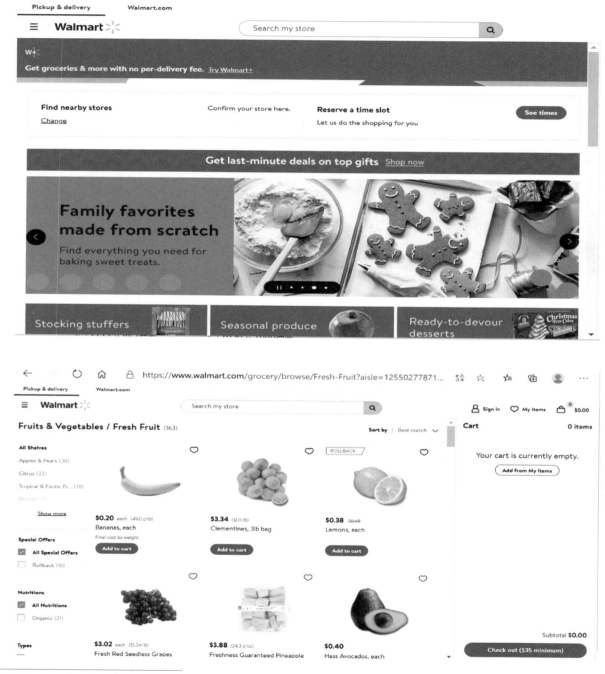

1 https://www.walmart.com/grocery

☐ After you place your order, you can view it in your account. You can edit, cancel, or reschedule any time before the cutoff.

☐ Choose your pickup or delivery location.

☐ On the **Review Your Order** screen, you can update your location, phone number, and payment method. You can also manage your substitutions and add promo codes. When you're ready to place your order, tap or click **Place order**.

☐ Add items to your cart. Your shopping cart will show you the minimum order total you need to place an order.

☐ Tap or click **See times** to choose your pickup or delivery window.

☐ Add your payment method.

Written Orders

An order is a commercial document used to request a company to supply goods or services in return for payment. A written order can be sent by letter, fax or email. The information that should be included when placing an order is the customer's name and address, a description of the goods and the quantity requested, the price, delivery and payment details. It is also possible to add any conditions the order is **subject to**.

From:	John Wilde <john.wilde@wildeoptics.co.uk>
To:	Ken Liu <ken.liu@guangzhoulenses.com>
Sent:	4 March 20..
Subject:	Trial order
Attachments:	

Dear Mr Liu,

With reference to our **previous correspondence**, we would like to place a **trial order** as follows:

Men's sunglasses	No. 4550	100 pieces	@USD 35.00/**piece**
Women's sunglasses	No. 4580	50 pieces	@USD 42.00/piece
Unisex sunglasses	No. 4600	20 pieces	@USD 50.00/piece

The delivery and payment terms are **as per** your email dated 27th February 20.. . Please make sure the goods are packed in **plywood crates**, clearly marked with our company name and address.

We look forward to receiving your **pro-forma invoice**.

Yours sincerely,
John Wilde

Order Forms and Online Orders

Orders can also be made by filling in **pre-printed order forms**, and **attaching** them **to an accompanying** email, letter or fax, as well as by completing an order form online. When ordering goods from a website the whole transaction—the **selection** of the goods and quantity, **authorisation** for payment, **delivery terms** and costs—is usually completed **in one go**. When you are a **registered user** of a website, it is possible to store all your details and use a **one-click ordering system** which makes the process even quicker.

BERTOLUCCI WHOLESALERS

179 West Street
London
NW1 7PL
www.bertolucci.com

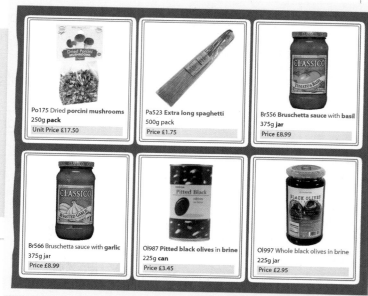

Po175 Dried **porcini** mushrooms 250g **pack** Unit Price £17.50	Pa523 Extra long spaghetti 500g pack Price £1.75
Br556 **Bruschetta sauce** with **basil** 375g **jar** Price £8.99	
Br566 Bruschetta sauce with **garlic** 375g jar Price £8.99	Ol987 **Pitted black olives** in **brine** 225g **can** Price £3.45
Ol997 Whole black olives in brine 225g jar Price £2.95	

CUSTOMER NAME

Nico's Italian Deli
17 New Cathedral Street
Manchester
Tel.: 0161 8956743
Fax: 0161 8956312
Email: gianni@bellaitalia.co.uk

ORDER NO.	897
DATE	8th September 20..

CUSTOMER ACCOUNT

No. 1579

DELIVERY ADDRESS

AS ABOVE

CODE	DESCRIPTION	QUANTITY	UNIT PRICE	TOTAL
(1) _____	Dried porcini mushrooms	(2) _____	£17.50	£262.50
Pa523	(3) _____	12	(4) _____	£21.00
Br556	(5) _____	20	£8.99	(6) _____
(7) _____	Pitted black olives	9	(8) _____	£31.05
			TOTAL	£494.35

selection	n.	选择	extra long spaghetti		超长意大利面
authorisation	n.	授权, 委托; 批准, 准许	bruschetta sauce		意式烤面包酱
delivery terms		运输条款	basil	n.	罗勒; 九层塔
in one go		一次; 一下子, 一口气	jar	n.	罐; 坛; 广口瓶
registered user		注册用户	garlic	n.	大蒜
one-click ordering system			pitted	adj.	去核的
		一键式订购系统	black olive	n.	黑橄榄
porcini mushrooms		牛肝菌	brine	n.	卤水, 盐水
pack	n.	袋	can	n.	罐; 筒; 听

2 Read the email and decide if the sentences are true (*T*) or false (*F*). If there is not enough information, choose "doesn't say" (*DS*).

	T	F	DS
1) John Wilde has done business with this company before.	☐	☐	☐
2) He orders a total of 170 items.	☐	☐	☐
3) The delivery terms were indicated in a previous email.	☐	☐	☐
4) The payment will be made after the goods are dispatched.	☐	☐	☐
5) The email contains instructions for how the goods should be packed.	☐	☐	☐
6) John Wilde does not request any other documents.	☐	☐	☐

3 Match the two halves of the sentences.

1) We thank you for
2) We are pleased to
3) We would be grateful if
4) The goods should be
5) We accept
6) If you are unable to
7) Please note that this order is
8) Thank you in advance for

a ☐ your prompt handling of this order.
b ☐ accept these terms, we shall be obliged to cancel our order.
c ☐ subject to delivery by 18th March.
d ☐ place an order for ski clothing.
e ☐ your quotation of 11th September.
f ☐ the payment and delivery terms indicated in your email.
g ☐ packed in wooden crates and marked with our company name.
h ☐ you could offer us a 5% discount on this order.

4 **Look at the order form and catalogue in Reading 1 and fill in the missing information in the table.**

1) _____   5) _____

2) _____   6) _____

3) _____   7) _____

4) _____   8) _____

5 **Now answer the questions.**

1) What type of company is Bertolucci?

_____

2) Who is the client and do you think this is the first time they have ordered from Bertolucci?

_____

3) What products do they order?

_____

4) What is the total cost of their order?

_____

Reading 2

Phone Orders

Orders can be made by phone directly to the **Sales Department** of a company. This is common when the customer has some questions to be answered or wants to check **availability** of a particular product. With phone orders, it is usually necessary to also send a written **confirmation**.

Accepting or Refusing an Order

After receiving an order, the seller may **acknowledge** the order or, under particular **circumstances**, refuse it. Reasons for **refusal** can include the **temporary unavailability** or **discontinuation** of an item, the impossibility to satisfy delivery **deadlines** or unacceptable discount or payment requests.

An order acknowledgement should:
• thank the customer for the order;
• **summarise** the details of the order;
• give any necessary explanation, e.g. special discounts, delivery, availability;
• end with a positive **reference** to this and future business.

A refusal letter should:

- **refer to** the customer's order;
- explain the reasons for the refusal;
- make a **counteroffer**, if suitable, e.g. offer an alternative item;
- end with a positive reference to future business.

Order Acknowledgement:

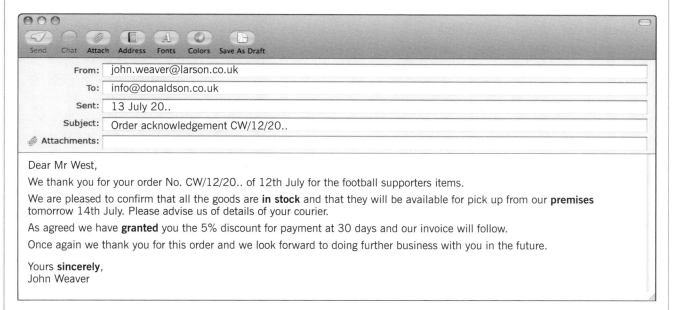

From: john.weaver@larson.co.uk
To: info@donaldson.co.uk
Sent: 13 July 20..
Subject: Order acknowledgement CW/12/20..
Attachments:

Dear Mr West,

We thank you for your order No. CW/12/20.. of 12th July for the football supporters items.

We are pleased to confirm that all the goods are **in stock** and that they will be available for pick up from our **premises** tomorrow 14th July. Please advise us of details of your courier.

As agreed we have **granted** you the 5% discount for payment at 30 days and our invoice will follow.

Once again we thank you for this order and we look forward to doing further business with you in the future.

Yours **sincerely**,
John Weaver

Refusal Letter

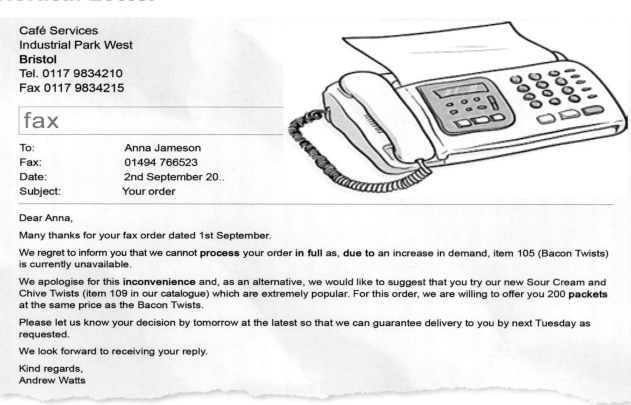

Café Services
Industrial Park West
Bristol
Tel. 0117 9834210
Fax 0117 9834215

fax

To: Anna Jameson
Fax: 01494 766523
Date: 2nd September 20..
Subject: Your order

Dear Anna,

Many thanks for your fax order dated 1st September.

We regret to inform you that we cannot **process** your order **in full** as, **due to** an increase in demand, item 105 (Bacon Twists) is currently unavailable.

We apologise for this **inconvenience** and, as an alternative, we would like to suggest that you try our new Sour Cream and Chive Twists (item 109 in our catalogue) which are extremely popular. For this order, we are willing to offer you 200 **packets** at the same price as the Bacon Twists.

Please let us know your decision by tomorrow at the latest so that we can guarantee delivery to you by next Tuesday as requested.

We look forward to receiving your reply.

Kind regards,
Andrew Watts

Sales Department		销售部	refer to		涉及; 关于; 参考; 指的是	
availability	*n.*	可用性; 有效性				
confirmation	*n.*	确认书	counteroffer	*n.*	还价; 还盘	
acknowledge	*v.*	确认, 承认, 认可; 确认收悉	in stock		有存货; 现有	
			premise	*n.*	厂区; 生产场所; 经营厂址	
circumstance	*n.*	情况; 条件	grant	*v.*	同意, 准予; 授予	
refusal	*n.*	拒绝, 回绝	sincerely	*adv.*	真诚地, 诚实地	
temporary	*adj.*	暂时的, 临时的; 短暂的	Bristol	*n.*	布里斯托尔 (英国西部的港口城市)	
unavailability	*n.*	不可获得; 无效用; 不适用				
			process	*v.*	处理, 办理	
discontinuation	*n.*	中止, 停止, 废止	in full		完整; 全额	
deadline	*n.*	最后期限, 截止日期	due to		由于, 归因于	
summarise	*n.*	概述, 概括, 总结	inconvenience	*n.*	不便, 麻烦	
reference	*n.*	参考, 参照; 涉及, 提到	packet	*n.*	小包; 小盒; 小袋	

6 **Read the order acknowledgement and the refusal letter in the text and underline the sentences/parts which correspond to the following instruction.**

An order acknowledgement should:

- thank the customer for the order;

- summarise the details of the order;

- give any necessary explanation, e.g. special discounts, delivery, availability;

- end with a positive reference to this and future business.

A refusal letter should:

- refer to the customer's order;

- explain the reasons for the refusal;

- make a counteroffer, if suitable, e.g. offer an alternative item;

- end with a positive reference to future business.

7 **Translate the order in Reading 2 acknowledgement and refusal letter into Chinese.**

1) Order acknowledgement

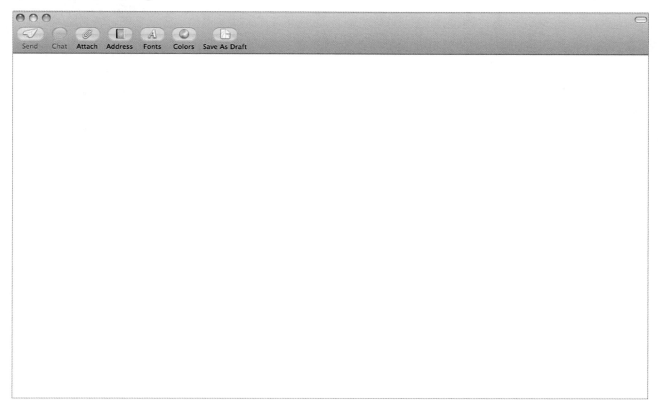

2) Refusal letter

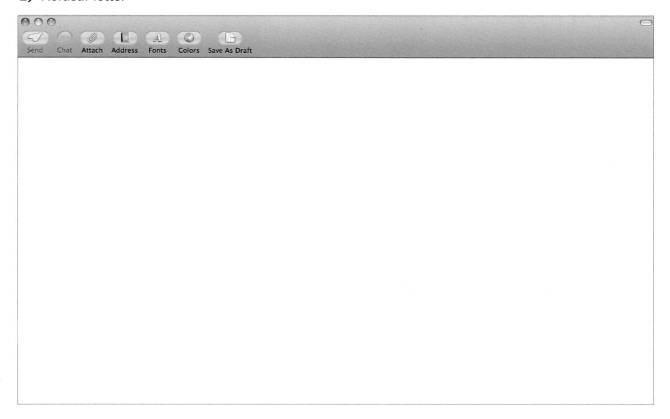

8 Read the email and put the sentences in the correct order.

From: Simon Howard <simon.howard@gseelectronics.com>

To: Roger Page <r.page@thedvdshop.co.uk>

Sent: 29 October 20..

Subject: Your order 156/200

Attachments:

Dear Mr Page,

☐ We sincerely regret any inconvenience and hope to receive further orders from you in the future.

☐ With reference to your above order for 20 portable DVD players, we are writing to inform you that unfortunately we cannot confirm your order.

☐ In this way we can process your order as quickly as possible.

☐ The expected delivery time would be approximately 6 weeks.

☐ Due to circumstances beyond our control, we are not able to deliver the items within two weeks as requested.

☐ If these terms are still suitable, please let us know.

Yours sincerely,
Simon Howard

9 Now answer the questions according to the above email.

1) What did Mr Page order?

2) When did he want the items delivered?

3) Why can not the order be processed?

4) Does Mr Howard offer an alternative?

Listening

10 Listen to the passage and complete the expressions.

Checking details	Making requests
Let me just (1) _____ that to you.	Could you tell me if model XYZ is available?
You said model ABC in blue, didn't you?	Can you (5) _____ me the item number, please?
Did you say 13 or 30?	Would you mind (6) _____ confirmation by fax?
Sorry, I didn't (2) _____ that.	**Making a promise**
Placing an order	Don't worry. I'll do it now.
I'd like to (3) _____ an order.	We'll (7) _____ the goods to you by next Thursday.
Can you (4) _____ my order?	I'll (8) _____ you back straightaway.
I'm phoning to order…	

11 Listen to three customers who call Katie Barnett in the Sales Department of QuikPrint, a supplier of ink cartridges for printers and photocopiers. Complete the missing information.

Customer: Siobhan, Samuels Ltd
Copier: Xerox (1) _____
Quantity: (2) _____
Price: £(3) _____
Delivery: (4) _____

New Customer: (5) _____
Sykes, Wainwright
Ink cartridges for
(6) _____, model (7) _____
Quantity: (8) _____
Email will follow

Todd Butler from (9) _____ Services
Printer/copier supplies for (10) _____
in the South East
Email with exact (11) _____ will follow
Has requested payment (12) _____ from
date of invoice

Writing

12 Write another letter from Mr Howard to Mr Page (see Exercise 8) in which:

— you thank him for his order

— you apologise and inform him the portable DVD model PVP 720 he requests is not in production

— you offer PVP 1020 instead and attach a brochure

— you ask for a confirmation email

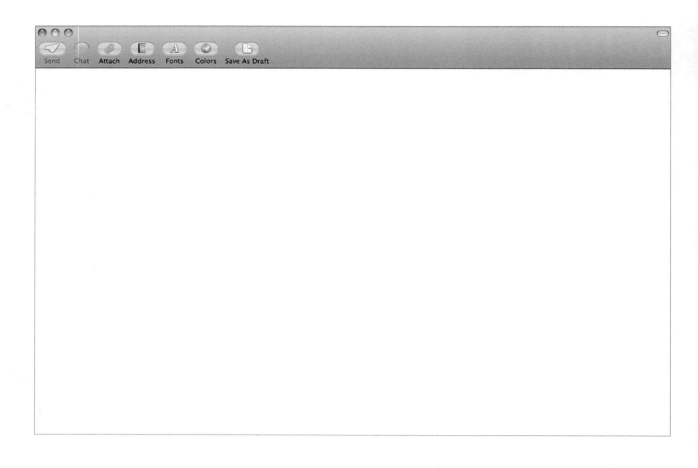

Speaking

13 **Practise this phone conversation in pairs. Then swap roles.**

Seller	Buyer
You work in the Sales Department of Kitchen Maid and you receive a phone call from Kathy's Kitchens. All your items are available immediately except for S124 which will be available in two weeks' time. You deliver by courier all over the country.	You work at Kathy's Kitchens, a shop selling kitchen and cooking equipment. You have seen Kitchen Maid's website and would like to place an order. Select the items you wish to purchase from the catalogue and phone Kitchen Maid's Sales Department to place your order.

Item No.	Description	Price
S124	20 cm kitchen knife	€23,99
F124	15 cm kitchen knife	€19,99
K178	vegetable peeler	€6,50
M870	lemon zester	€8,25

Technical Terms

1 **Purchase order**, or PO, is an official document issued by a buyer committing to pay the seller for the sale of specific products or services to be delivered in the future.

2 **Order acknowledgement**, or OA, is a written confirmation of an order which is sent by the producing or service rendering company that accepts the order placed by a customer.

3 **Agreement** is any understanding or arrangement reached between two or more parties.

4 **Contract** is a specific type of agreement that is legally binding, finalized through the signatures of both parties.

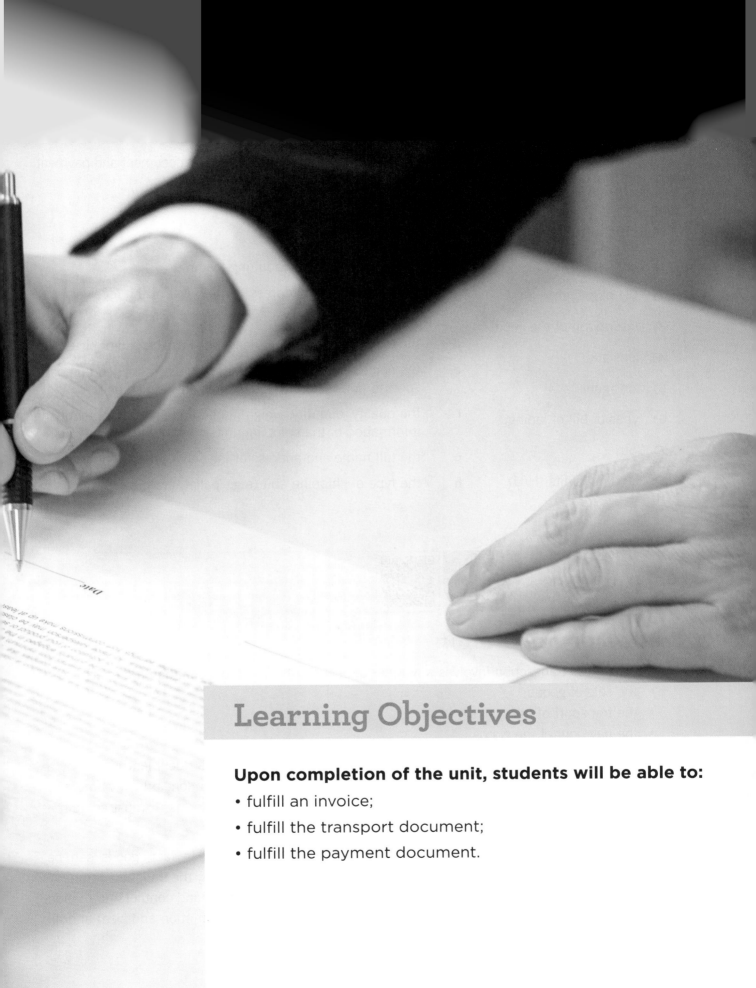

Learning Objectives

Upon completion of the unit, students will be able to:

- fulfill an invoice;
- fulfill the transport document;
- fulfill the payment document.

Starting Off

In this unit you may be studying trade documentation, such as invoice, transport document and payment document. But do you know the items in detail?

1 **Match the following items with the explanation.**

1) Date	a ☐ the number of units requiring loading
2) H/U pkg. type	b ☐ the full name and address of the buyer or the receiver
3) Description of the goods	c ☐ the transport company
4) Consigner	d ☐ the month, day and year the freight was shipped or picked up
5) Consignee	e ☐ the notes such as "received for shipment" "shipped on board" "port to port" "clean" "foul" "claused" and so on
6) Types of bill of lading	f ☐ the quality, quantity, weight, condition and other identifying information of the shipping units
7) Carrier	g ☐ the full name and address of the seller or the sender
8) Handling Units (H/U)	h ☐ the type of shipping unit (e.g., pallet, crate, drum, carton)

Reading 1

Trade Documentation

Any business transaction involves a number of documents. The most common are related to:
- the sale of goods;
- the transport of the goods;
- the payment of the goods.

The document related to the sale of goods is called an invoice. It is a document **issued** by a seller to a buyer and it shows details of the goods sold (quantity, description, price), name and contact information of both the seller and the buyer, as well as payment terms. It must contain a number and a date.

The transport document depends on the means of transport used. In fact, goods can be transported by train, by **lorry**, by ship or by plane. This document is issued by the transport company which takes the goods and delivers them to the buyer. It contains the name and contact information of the seller, the buyer and the **carrier**, details of the goods (quantity, description and size) and all information about when and where the goods leave and arrive.

Payments involve banks that move money from the buyer's **bank account** to the seller's bank account. One of the most frequently used means is the **bank transfer**.

The choice of which payment terms to use in a business transaction depends on different factors. One factor is the relationship between the seller and the buyer because some means of payment can be safer for the seller: for example, payment in advance, which means that the buyer pays before receiving the goods. On the other hand, the means of payment that gives the **maximum security** to the buyer but represents the greatest risk to the seller is **open account terms** in which the buyer agrees to pay the seller's invoice at a future date, usually in 30 to 90 days. This means of payment is used only if the buyer is financially **reliable** and the seller trusts him.

MY GLOSSARY

issue	v.	开具; 发行; 颁发
lorry	n.	货车
carrier	n.	承运人; 运输工具
bank account		银行账户
bank transfer		银行汇款; 银行间转账

maximum	adj.	最大的; 最高的, 顶点的
security	n.	安全保障; 保护措施
open account terms		赊账交易条件; 记账方式交易
reliable	adj.	可信赖的

2 Answer the questions.

1) What document refers to the sale of goods?
2) Who issues it?
3) How many means of transport can you think of?
4) Can you give a definition of carrier?
5) What does payment in advance consist of?
6) When does a buyer usually pay on open account terms?

3 Look at this table. Tick (√) the documents where you can find these elements.

	Invoice	Transport Document	Payment Document
Buyer's name			
Seller's name			
Carrier's name			
Details of the goods			
Name of bank			

4 Translate the following sentences into Chinese.

1) The document related to the sale of goods is called an invoice. It is a document issued by a seller to a buyer and it shows details of the goods sold (quantity, description, price), name and contact information of both the seller and the buyer, as well as payment terms.

_____

_____

2) The transport document depends on the means of transport used. In fact, goods can be transported by train, by lorry, by ship or by plane. This document is issued by the transport company which takes the goods and delivers them to the buyer.

_____

_____

3) Payments involve banks that move money from the buyer's bank account to the seller's bank account. One of the most frequently used means is the bank transfer.

_____

_____

5 Match the documents on the left to the definitions on the right.

1) B/L (Bill of Lading)

a ☐ a written order used primarily in international trade that binds one party to pay a fixed sum of money to another party on demand or at a predetermined date

2) Insurance Policy

b ☐ a commercial document issued by a seller to a buyer, relating to a sale transaction and indicating the products, quantities, and agreed prices for products or services the seller had provided the buyer

3) Invoice

c ☐ a document declaring in which country a commodity or good was manufactured

4) L/C (Letter of Credit)

d ☐ a legal document issued by a carrier to a shipper that details the type, quantity and destination of the goods being carried

5) Packing List

e ☐ a proof that what you are shipping is, in fact, what the customer ordered, and is also of good quality

6) Inspection Certificate of Quality

f ☐ a document that contains the agreement that an insurance company and a person have made

7) CO (Certificate of Origin)

g ☐ a document which details the contents, and often dimensions and weight, of each package or container

8) Bill of Exchange (Draft)

h ☐ a letter issued by a bank to another bank (typically in a different country) to serve as a guarantee for payments made to a specified person under specified conditions

Reading **2**

D&M Fashion is an English company that makes **accessories**. One of its customers, an Italian shop, has sent them an order. Let's look at the documents in the transaction.

The Invoice

D&M Fashion			Invoice No.: 45/A

D&M Fashion
www.dandm.com
15 Lockett Street
Manchester, M8 8EE
Tel.: 0161 8349652
Fax: 0161 8349655
info@dandm.com

Invoice No.: 45/A
Invoice Date: 14 April 2020

Order No.: 66/11
Order Date: 2 March 2020

Buyer: Nonsologioielli
Via Oriani 35
48121 **Ravenna**
Italy

Quantity	Art. No	Description	Unit Price	Total Price
40	A52	**ear ring**	£12.50	£500.00
50	A55	ear ring	£10.90	£545.00
35	G63	**ring**	£7.80	£273.00
65	H87	**bracelet**	£22.40	£1456.00
				Total: £2774.00

Payment Terms: bank transfer 30 days from invoice date

The Payment Document

As we know from the invoice above, Nonsologioielli has to pay by bank transfer 30 days from the date of the invoice.

Deutsche Bank
C.so Cavour 58
8121 Ravenna
Italy

Customer's name: Nonsologioielli
IBAN IT57S0100503392000000218192
BIC: BDMRIT3GXXX

Amount to pay: £2774.00
Reference: Invoice No. 45/A of 14/04/2020

Beneficiary's name: D&M FASHION
Beneficiary's IBAN: GB15400515128834735678
Bank name: **Allied** Banks **plc**
BIC: ALBS8355XXX

accessory	n.	配饰；附件，配件
Manchester	n.	曼彻斯特（英格兰西北部一大城市）
Ravenna	n.	拉文那（意大利东北部港市）
ear ring		耳环；耳饰
ring	n.	戒指；环状物
bracelet	n.	手镯，手链

IBAN (International Bank Account Number)	abbr.	国际银行账号
BIC (Bank Identification Code)	abbr.	银行识别码
beneficiary	n.	受益人
allied	adj.	联盟的
plc (public limited company)	abbr.	公共股份有限公司

6 **Look at the invoice in Reading 2 and answer the questions.**

1) What's the exporter's name?

2) What's the importer's name?

3) Where are the two companies based?

4) When is the invoice issued?

5) When did the buyer send his order?

6) What are the invoice and the order numbers?

7) How many different types of articles does the buyer buy?

8) What is the most expensive article?

9) How does the buyer pay?

10) What is the total amount of the invoice?

7 **Complete this text summarising the invoice in Reading 2.**

This document is a(n) (1) _____ sent by (2) _____ to one of its customers called (3) _____. The invoice is issued on (4) _____ 2020 and it refers to order No. (5) _____ of (6) _____ 2020. The Italian customer buys earrings, (7) _____ and (8) _____ for a total quantity of (9) _____ items and for a total amount of (10) £ _____.

8 **Look at the bank transfer issued by their bank. What do IBAN and BIC stand for? Use some of the words in the box.**

number	amount	international	customer	account
identification	identifier	nation	code	bank

IBAN: _____

BIC: _____

9 **Complete the sentences which describe the payment document in Reading 2.**

1) This document is a(n)

_____

2) It is issued by

_____

3) This bank transfer is ordered by

_____

4) The bank transfer is for the amount of

_____

5) This amount refers to

_____

6) The bank that receives the amount is

_____

7) The English bank transfers the amount to the account of

_____

10 Listen to the dialogue between Diana Downing and her colleague Bob who work for the courier transporting the goods ordered by Nonsologioielli. They are writing the air waybill. Complete the air waybill.

	406 – 0000 0000
Consignor's name: (1) _____ 15 Lockett Street Manchester, M8 8EE	548 – 4310 – 9022 Air waybill issued by: UK World Courier 72 Maple Road Manchester M3 2BY
Consignee's name: Nonsologioielli Via Oriani 35 (2) _____ Ravenna Italy	

Airport of **departure**: (3) _____	Airport of **destination**: (4) _____

Flight no.: BA 399	Flight Date: (5) _____ 2020

No. of **packages** (6) _____	**Gross weight** (7) _____ ,80kg	Nature and Quantity of Goods (including dimensions or volume) 1 box 40cm x 30cm x 15cm

Signature of Issuing Carrier: *Diana Downing* _____	Date: (8) _____ /04/2020

N.O.3
ORIGINAL FOR **SHIPPER** 406 – 0000 0000

11 Listen to the dialogue again, and find the following information.

1) The number of the air waybill and date issued:

_____

2) The name of the courier:

_____

3) Where the goods leave from:

_____

4) When the goods leave:

_____

5) Where the goods arrive:

_____

6) The number of boxes, their weight and dimensions:

_____

Writing

12 Suppose you are a staff of D&M Fashion. Fill in the invoice No.98/A according to the following order No.89/21 on 19 Jan. 2020.

Tianjin Hetian Import and Export Corp.
35 Weijin Road
Nankai District
Tianjin 300071
China
Tel: +86-022-6467-3474
Fax: +86-022-6457-3475
11 Jan. 2020

Order No.: 89/21

D&M Fashion
15 Lockett Street Manchester, M8 8EE

Dear Sirs:

We wish to thank you for your offer of 5 Jan. 2020 offering us 100 H98 silver bracelets at £135.60 per piece. We find your offer satisfactory and are pleased to give you trial order for the following items:

Description	Art. No.	Quantity	Unit Price	Total
Silver Bracelets	H98	100 pieces	£135.60	£13,560.00
Total				£13,560.00

Our usual terms of payment are by transfer 30 days from invoice date.
We hope to place further and large orders with you in the near future.
We are looking forward to your early reply.

Yours sincerely,
Wang Lin
Import and Export department
Tianjin Hetian Import and Export Corp.

D&M Fashion
www.dandm.com
15 Lockett Street
Manchester, M8 8EE
Tel.: 0161 8349652
Fax: 0161 8349655
info@dandm.com

Invoice No.: (2)
Invoice Date: (3)

Order No.: (4)
Order Date: (5)

Buyer: (1)

Quantity	Art. No	Description	Unit Price	Total Price
(6)	(7)	(8)	(9)	(10)
				Total: (11)

Payment Terms: bank transfer 30 days from invoice date

13 Discuss the differences of payment by L/C and payment by remittance. Then choose one of the team members to make a presentation on behalf of your team.

Technical Terms

1 **Transaction documents** are a series of documents provided by the seller or the buyer or any other related third par in order to fulfill the transaction.

2 **Invoice** is a document issued by a seller to the buyer that indicates the quantities and price of the products or services provided by the seller.

3 **Air waybill** (AWB), also known as air consignment note, is a document that accompanies goods shipped by an international air courier to provide detailed information about the shipment.

4 **Bank transfer** is the process or action of moving money from one bank account to another with detailed document acted as a confirmation of payment.

Learning Objectives

Upon completion of the unit, students will be able to:

- outline job application process;
- write application email and personal CV for a position;
- understand common questions in job interviews and give proper answers.

Starting Off

When you finish university, you will look for a job. In this unit you may be studying job application. The first step will be contacting the company you want to work for. But do you know exactly how to write a job application which is a proposal to work for them?

1 **The application process involves different steps. How do you think this process works? Put the steps in the correct order.**

☐ The company reads your application, thinks you could be the right person and contacts you for an interview.

☐ You accept and start working for them.

☐ They contact you and offer you the job.

☐ You go to the interview.

☐ You send your application.

☐ You read an advertisement in which a company looks for a computer programmer.

☐ Your interview is successful.

We can say that the three main steps in the application process are:

1) Advertisement

2) Application

3) Interview

First Step: The Advertisement

Job advertisements can be found on the Internet, on special sites or on company sites, but also in newspapers and magazines.

Ads

JOB: bank **cashier**
COMPANY: Walkers Bank
LOCATION: Boston
Walkers Bank
TERMS: Permanent / Full-time
DUTIES: customer service and **administrative** duties
EDUCATION: high school **diploma**
SKILLS: good knowledge of banking computer systems

Click here to apply or send an email plus CV
to Staff Manager, walkersbank@wb.org

Experienced café **staff**
needed to work at
Party Café in Manchester.
Party Café

You will be required to work
from the end of November
till the 23rd December.
There are **various shifts** and times **available**.
Many of the shifts are in the evening allowing
you to work around your studies or another job.

Part time **vacancies** available.

Email your application and CV to
jobs@cafebar.uk

MY GLOSSARY

cashier	n.	出纳员
administrative	adj.	管理的; 行政的
diploma	n.	毕业文凭; 文凭课程
staff	n.	全体职工; (学校) 行政人员

various	adj.	各种不同的, 各种各样的
shift	n.	轮班; 改变
vacancy	n.	(职位) 空缺, 空职; 空房

2 Read the two advertisements and answer the questions.

1) Which job is better for a student?

2) Which job is full-time only?

3) Which job is not permanent? When are you required to work?

4) Which job does not require a school diploma?

5) How can you apply for both of them?

3 Fill in the form with the abbreviations and Chinese translations of the terms.

Term	Abbreviation	Chinese
1) advertisement		
2) Curriculum Vitae		
3) corporation		
4) part time		
5) full time		
6) one thousand		
7) department		
8) Monday-Friday		
9) words per minute		
10) over time		

4 Complete the sentences with the abbreviations in the above form.

1) There are 8 staff in the HR _____.

2) I have known your name and address from the _____ in the newspaper.

3) My average speed went from roughly 80 _____, to over 120 after practice.

4) Most of us work for 8 hours a day, _____.

5) You'd better enclose your _____ with the application letter.

5 **Match the job titles on the left to the job descriptions on the right.**

1) Receptionist

a ☐ dealing with international clients and searching for suitable sales trade opportunities within the company and from the clients abroad

2) International Documentation Specialist

b ☐ assisting in organising marketing campaigns, planning marketing strategies and tracking marketing programs

3) Secretary

c ☐ placing job ads on careers pages, updating employee records and assisting in payroll preparation

4) International Sales Representative

d ☐ preparing documentation for exportation to the foreign country, customs clearance and payment collection for all applicable parties

5) HR clerk

e ☐ handling correspondence and manage routine and detail work for a superior

6) Marketing Assistant

f ☐ answering calls and fielding them accordingly, addressing visitor questions and needs, and providing an overall welcoming environment

Second Step: The Application

After reading a job advertisement, if you are interested in the job, you send your application, usually by email. Your application must include a CV (Curriculum Vitae). This is a document with information about you and your work history. A CV must be clear and easy to read, so it must be organised into sections.

Applications

(1) _____

Dear Staff Manager,

(2) _____

I am writing to apply for the post of bank cashier advertised on your site.

(3) _____

As you can see from my CV, I got a high school diploma in 2009. Since then I have been working as a bank cashier for a major bank here in Boston where I deal with customers' accounts and sell financial products.

(4) _____

I hope you will contact me for an interview.

(5) _____

Best regards,

Paul Ascott

Dear Sirs,

(6) _____

I saw your advert on your site and I am interested in the post of bank cashier.

(7) _____

I hope you will appreciate both my educational qualifications—I have a degree in Economics from Boston University—and my two years' experience in the field of banking.

(8) _____

My computer skills are excellent and I can speak Russian well.

(9) _____

I attach my CV and two references.

(10) _____

I look forward to meeting you for an interview.

(11) _____

Regards,

Mary Burton

CVs

PERSONAL DETAILS
NAME: Paul Ascott
DATE OF BIRTH: 3/11/1991
ADDRESS: 15 Park Avenue,
Boston
PHONE NO. 359 992177
EMAIL: paul.ascott@gmail.com

EDUCATION
2004-2009 High School Diploma—
High School West, Boston

PROFESSIONAL EXPERIENCE
2009—present Atlantic Bank,
163 High Street, Boston—bank
cashier
Duties: dealing with customers'
accounts,
selling financial products

SKILLS
good knowledge of standard office
software

PERSONAL INFORMATION
Ms Mary Burton
Born in Boston on 15th June 1986
Married
35 San Diego Rd – Boston
(617) 466 2481
mburton@hotmail.com

EDUCATION
High School: 2000 – 2005 Parker High School, Boston
University: 2005 – 2009 Degree in Economics, Boston University

EMPLOYMENT
2009 – present   investment consultant at DT Bank—I assist customers in
                  investments

SKILLS
Languages: Good Russian both written and spoken
Computer: Certificate in Microsoft Office

REFERENCES	George Brown	Gordon O'Neal
	Teacher of Economics	Manager
	Boston University	DT Bank State Street
	(617) 455 6002	(617) 430 8832
	gbrown@bu.com	gordononeal@dtbank.com

Third Step: The Interview

If your application is successful, the company will contact you for an interview before deciding whether to give you the job.

6 Look at the items of information from a CV and put them in the appropriate sections.

— Excellent English both written and spoken

— Email: c.parker@topmail.com

— 2008-present: accountant at French Foods, 11 Avenue St Antoine, Nantes

— M. Gaston Artois, Directeur Général at French Foods

— 2007: High school diploma in accountancy from Lycée Saint-Louis, Tours

Section	Information
Personal information	
Work experience	
Education	
Skills	
References	

7 Two people have decided to apply for the post of bank cashier from the first advertisement in Reading 1. Read the two applications in Reading 2 and fill in the blanks with the help of the words and phrases in the box. Be noted that some of them can be reused.

attachments	education	work experience	skills
references	closing	salutation (opening greeting)	
opening (source of information + type of job)		hope for interview	

(1) _____

(2) _____

(3) _____

(4) _____

(5) _____

(6) _____

(7) _____

(8) _____

(9) _____

(10) _____

(11) _____

8 Complete the sentences with words or phrases from the box.

apply	application	deal with	attach	look forward to
interview	advertisement	duties	skills	knowledge

1) I _____ copies of my diplomas.

2) I have good _____ of French and Italian.

3) My _____ include organising meetings and events and advertising.

4) I would like to _____ for the post of computer programmer.

5) I saw your _____ in The Daily Telegraph and I am applying for the post of secretary.

6) I _____ your reply.

7) I am available for a(n) _____ at any time.

8) In my present job, I _____ accounts.

9) Excellent computer _____ are required.

10) Please send your _____ to this email address.

9 Please look at the CVs that Paul Ascott and Mary Burton have attached to their applications in Reading 2. Read them and tick (√) the table appropriately.

Who:	Paul Ascott	Mary Burton
has a degree?		
is still working?		
does not provide any references?		
can speak a foreign language?		
is married?		
has experience as a bank cashier?		
can use a computer?		
lives in Boston?		

Listening

10 This is a list of typical questions during a job interview. First match the topics in the box to the questions. Then listen to an interview and match proper answers a–j to the questions. There may be more than one answer for each question.

Skills	Work experience	Education	Interest in the job

Questions

1) What are your qualifications? *Education e, f*

2) What school did you attend? _____

3) Tell me about your experience. _____

4) What work experience have you got? _____

5) What are your duties? _____

6) What experience have you got in this field? _____

7) Do you speak any foreign languages? _____

8) What are your computer skills and what programs can you use? _____

9) Why do you want this job? _____

10) What interests you about this job? _____

Answers

a I am familiar with all the main computer programs.

b I have a good knowledge of computers.

c I think this job will improve my skills.

d I want to get experience in this field.

e   I have a diploma in accountancy (and a degree in Economics).

f   I went to ITC Pascoli in Milan and got my diploma 3 years ago.

g   I worked for an import-export company called BC Ltd. from 2008 to 2010.

h   I have several years of office experience.

i   I am responsible for/My duties are entering data into the computer and preparing statistical reports.

j   Yes, I can speak English fluently.

11 **Listen to Michael Green's interview for a job as an office clerk and decide if the statements are true (*T*) or false (*F*). Correct the false statements.**

1)   Michael is 32.

2)   He finished school 2 months ago.

3)   He was a shop assistant in a sports store.

4)   He has been working as a clerk since he stopped working for SportCentre.

5)   He wants to leave his job because he wants to improve his office skills.

6)   In his present job he does not use a computer.

7)   He has no experience of office work.

8)   He is good with computers.

9)   He can't speak Italian.

10) He will be contacted in a couple of months.

Writing

12 **Now, you have decided to apply for the post of a bank cashier. Write your application email and CV using the information below. Use the layout and vocabulary from the emails and CVs in this unit for your help.**

— you have read the advertisement on the Internet

— you are 25, from Boston

— you have a high school diploma

— after school you worked for 3 years as a representative for a videogame company, then for 2 years as a bank clerk with administrative duties for a bank in Boston

— you have excellent computer knowledge

— you attach 1 reference

Speaking

13 Now imagine you have applied for a job as a shop assistant in a music shop in London. Complete your interview with the missing words and phrases.

Interviewer:	Good morning and welcome.
You:	(1) _____ .
Interviewer:	I'd like to ask you a few questions. Let's start with education. What (2) _____ qualifications?
You:	I (3) _____ .
Interviewer:	Fine. And (4) _____ in this field?
You:	I (5) _____ .
Interviewer:	Can you tell me about your computer (6) _____ ?
You:	(7) _____ .
Interviewer:	That's great. Now, you can speak good English, but can you speak any other (8) _____ ?
You:	I (9) _____ .
Interviewer:	I see. Now, one last question. Why (10) _____ ?
You:	(11) _____ .
Interviewer:	OK. That's all for now. Thank you for coming. We'll contact you soon.
You:	Thank you very much.

Technical Terms

1 CV (Curriculum Vitae) is a short document that describes your education, qualification, work experience, etc.

2 Duty refers to something that you have to do as part of your job.

3 Reference is a formal recommendation by someone who knows you well to a potential future employer about your abilities, dependability, etc. It also refers to a person who writes this recommendation.

4 Attachment is a file or document that is attached to a message or an email.

5 Certificate is an official document that you receive when you have completed a course of study or training.